Who is this Jesus?

By

Barr. Favour Victory

Barr. Favour Victory

First Printing: May 2020
Quiver Publishers Inc.
www.quiverpublishers.com.ng

Dedication

This book is dedicated to our Lord Jesus Christ whose sacrifice and love brought salvation to me and mankind

Acknowledgement

I hereby acknowledge the power of the Holy Spirit and Grace of God that enabled me to write this book. To God be the glory.

I also appreciate Engr. Clement.C.Okoli who helped in proofreading this book and my valuable wife Mrs. Gloria Victoria.

<u>TABLE OF CONTENT</u>

CHAPTER ONE

DIVINE REVELATION

"Wherefore God also hath highly exalted him and given him a name which is above every name: That at the name of Jesus every knee should bow of things in heaven and things in earth and things under the earth; And that every tongue should confess that Jesus Christ is Lord, to the glory of God the Father". Philippians 2:9-11.

Apostle Paul, one of the greatest writers of the Bible with wonderful spiritual experiences speaking in the same vain have this as a personal deep desire "That I may know Him and the power of his resurrection and the fellowship of his sufferings being made conformable unto his death". Mathew 16:13.

Before we look at the answer given by Jesus disciples, we need to understand that it was not only asking Jesus the question. The people of Jerusalem were in dare need of answer to who is this Jesus. At the time Jesus was about rounding up his ministry and he was moving towards Jerusalem, the people marveled at the kind of impromptu response and reception given to Jesus and they needed an answer to their question. And the multitude that went before, and that followed cried, saying Hosannah to the son of David: Blessed is he that cometh in the name of the Lord; Hosannah in the highest". And when he was come into Jerusalem, all the city was moved, saying, who is this? Mathew 21:9-10.

The question who is this Jesus did not end here because spectacular event was following Jesus through his ministry in earlier event before triumphant entry, the same question came up when nature submitted to his command. And they feared exceedingly and said one to another "What manner of man is this, that even the wind and the sea obey him? – Mark 4:41.

Our concern is that you should know in proper perspective who Jesus is, because if you depend upon people's opinion or knowledge about Jesus, you may not know properly who Jesus is or you may have a parochial knowledge or understanding of Jesus.

Depending upon the opinion of any man who is not spiritually linked with heaven cannot in all standard give you a proper idea of who Jesus is. The person who gives you the information may be a believer, a pastor, a disciple, a minister or even founding pastor of a church or ministry. The position or title of that man or woman is not important. The most important thing is if the person is divinely connected to receive knowledge about who Jesus is.

In the book of Ps. 1:1 for example the bible state, "Blessed is the man that walketh not in the counsel of the ungodly…" you discovered that knowledge may come from godly person but has no bearing or God is not the source. This counsel can only be qualified as a counsel of the ungodly. so it is important to know whom you believe or depend upon for proper knowledge about who Jesus is.

It is also necessary to be properly informed about who Jesus is so that your opinion or understanding about Jesus that is dependent upon what others say about Jesus may not be misrepresented. In understanding who Jesus is you may not lean on your understanding that has no biblical support.

The disciples of Jesus gave Jesus answers of whom the people said He is "And they said some say that thou art John the Baptist, some, Elias; and others, Jeremiah or one of the prophets". Matt. 16:14.
Looking at the answers the disciples gave to Jesus about the people's opinion about Jesus, you will discover from your little

knowledge that the answers are not correct and can never be correct. Jesus can never be John the Baptist; John the Baptist was alive when Jesus ministry started so it will be foolish for anybody to think or believe that Jesus is the John the Baptist; Jesus also declared that John the Baptist is his own witness see John 5:32-33.

"There is another that beareth witness of me and I know that the witness which he witnesseth of me is true. Ye sent unto John, and he bare witness unto the truth". See verse 36.

Jesus is not Elijah, we remembered that during the transfiguration of our Lord Jesus, Elijah was present on the mountain when Jesus was present, he could not manifest himself in two different persons.

Though there are scriptures that made a link and reference between Jesus ministry and Elijah's ministry. It is necessary at this point to pause and consider it a little before we continue on this journey to discover who this Jesus is.

In the book of Malachi 4:5-6 "Behold I will send you Elijah the prophet before the coming of the great and dreadful day of the Lord: And he shall turn the heart of the fathers to the children and the heart of the children to their fathers, lest I come and smite the earth with a curse".

Before we expatiate on the scripture written above, it is important to know that in the scripture whenever **"Elias"** is used, this refers to Elijah, because Elias is the Greek form of Elijah.

Both John the Baptist and Elijah have a role destined that they must play in the ministry of our Lord Jesus Christ. Just as John the Baptist came to prepare the way for the coming of our Lord Jesus which was prophesied by Malachi in the book of Malachi 3:10 "Behold I will send my messenger, and he shall prepare the way before me and the Lord, whom ye seek shall suddenly come to his temple even, the messenger of the covenant, whom ye delight in, behold he shall come saith the Lord of hosts". Also in the book of Isaiah 40:3 "The voice of him that crieth in the wilderness, prepare ye the way of the Lord make straight in the desert a highway for our God".

The role of Elijah in the ministry of our Lord Jesus started with the transfiguration of our Lord Jesus and he is expected according to the prophecy in Malachi 4:5-6 to come before the second coming of our Lord Jesus Christ. Also the scripture in the book of Revelation 11:3-6.

"And I will give power unto my two witnesses and they shall prophecy a thousand two hundred and three score days, clothed in sackcloth.

These are the two olive trees and the two candlesticks standing before the God of the earth. And if any man will hurt them, fire proceedeth of their mouth and devoureth their enemies: and if any man will hurt them, he must in this manner be killed. These have power to shut heaven that it rain not in the days of their prophecy: and have power over waters to turn them to blood and to smite the earth with all plagues, as often as they will".

Although the bible recorded about two men who shut the heavens and there was no rain: They are Elisha and Elijah. But with the combination of Malachi 4:5-6 and Revelation 11:6 we discovered that the scriptures is referring to Elijah to be one of those witnesses that will come before the second coming of Jesus to the earth.

In Matthew 11:14 "And if ye will receive it, this is Elias, which was for to come". Jesus in this verse talking about John the Baptist also made reference to Elijah. The question is, is Jesus talking about re-incarnation. The Bible said "And as it is appointed unto men once to die, but after that the judgment" Hebrew 9:27, Death in the verse signifies a translation from this earth to either Heaven or Hell.

Though one may argue that Elijah did not die physically but it is true and obvious that he translated from this earth to heaven and nobody apart from Jesus during the transfiguration has seen Elijah anywhere in this world.

The Bible condemned the issue of re-incarnation and the word of God cannot contradict itself. Further in the book of Luke 1:13 and 17. "But the angel said unto him, fear not Zacharias for thy prayer is heard, and thy wife Elizabeth shall bear thee a son, and thou shall call his name John… and he shall go before him in the spirit and power of Elias, to turn the hearts of fathers to the children, and the disobedient to the wisdom of the just; to make ready a people prepared for the Lord. "This scripture bring to rest on the whole issue of re-incarnation. The scripture explains that John the Baptist shall operate in the same spirit and power which Elijah operated.

It means both shall work by the same power of the Holy Ghost and their pattern of ministry shall be the same. That is why you can see about 18 similarities between the ministry of John the Baptist and Elijah.

John the Baptist is a personality on his own who was destined to be Christ forerunner while Elijah is also a distinct personality from John the Baptist with a divine mandate to become a forerunner for the second coming of our Lord Jesus Christ, it means that Jesus is not John the Baptist neither is he Elijah.

The next person on line that the people taught Jesus to be according to Mathew 16:14 is Jeremiah. Jeremiah was a renowned prophet used by God to warn Israelites about the impending Judgment of God if they do not repent. Though he was a great prophet, his ministry is entirely different from Jesus ministry. This is because Jesus not only come to tell us to repent, he made himself a sacrifice for our sins and showed the people the way to salvation. Jesus in all ramifications is not Jeremiah. Jeremiah even in his ministry made reference to Jesus. Jeremiah 23:5,6 *"Behold the days come, saith the Lord that I will raise unto David a righteous Branch and a king shall reign and prosper and shall execute judgment and Justice in the earth. In his days Judah shall be saved and Israel shall dwell safely and this is His name whereby he shall be called, THE LORD OF RIGHTEOUSNESS"*.

The last sect of people who considered Jesus not to be John the Baptist, Elijah or Jeremiah said, as in Matthew 16:14 that he is one of the prophets. Though one may acknowledge that Jesus was a prophet, but he is beyond being one of the prophets because in his answer to the personality of John the Baptist whom He regarded as a prophet, He has this to say about John the Baptist in Luke 7:24, 28. *"And when the messengers of John were departed, He began to speak unto the people concerning John, what went ye out into the wilderness for to see? A reed shaken with the wind? For I say unto you, among those are born of women there is not a greater prophet than John the Baptist: but he that is least in the kingdom of God is greater than he"*.

If the above scripture is interpreted correctly and Jesus is declared to be one of the prophets then according to the word of Jesus, does it mean that John the Baptist is greater than Jesus since Jesus was born of a woman (according to the flesh)?

The word of God we know cannot contradict itself so the word of John the Baptist about Jesus is quite relevant now see John 3:28, 30, and 31. *"Ye yourselves bear me witness that I said, I am not the Christ, but that I am sent before him… He must increase, but I must decrease. He that cometh from above is above all: he that is of the earth is earthly and speaketh of the earth: he that cometh from heaven is above all"*.

It is quite obvious that John speaking according to the leading of the spirit recognized that Jesus is above him and he said whose sandal latchet he is not worthy to unloose.

The issue of regarding Jesus as Elias or one of the prophets did not start with him but by the people. It was the same case with John the Baptist, the people looking at the ministry of John the Baptist made reference to the coming of Elias.

The people were aware of the coming of the Messiah according to various prophecies in the Old Testament like Isaiah and Zechariah, so they were eager to identify or associate this prophecy with any prophet that came in the New Testament dispensation. But because their spiritual understanding was highly limited, they were not in link with God through the Holy Spirit hence they resorted to guess work. However guesswork has no place in spiritual matter or discernment of spirit.

Indeed there was a spiritual Lacuna between the period marking the end of the era of Malachi and the beginning of the era of the books of the New Testament. They were thirsty of the word of God. Because it was then scarce and everybody was waiting for the coming of the Messiah. But because they were not spiritually alert or had no spiritual consciousness they could not discern when the visitation of the Messiah would be.

In the ministry of Jesus He wept for Jerusalem because they did not know the time of their visitation.

It will be spiritual and material "**suicide**" for any person to lack spiritual understanding of the time of his divine visitation or the personality the Lord has positioned to use to bring his or her salvation.

The people of Israel were in this situation and had no option than to rely upon their guesswork. Such we know is very dangerous because one is bound to make mistakes.

It is important to know how God deals with you and probably the instrument or vessel He had prepared to use to bless you, many people have fallen into great problem because they went to wrong persons for salvations. It does not matter the level of your anointing, you need to constantly depend upon the Holy Spirit for direction. Even a big time prophet Samuel almost made the mistake in the selection of the second king in Israel. If not for the timely intervention of God that directed him to anoint David. This is because Samuel left the Holy Spirit and decided to work by sight.

People are easily moved by outward physical manifestation especially when they are not in tune with the working of the Holy Spirit.

The people of Israel were carried away by the manifestation of the ministry of John the Baptist and also the crowd that followed his ministry. In as much as crowd is quite important in ministry even as the bible recorded that multitude followed Jesus but ministry is not a crowd thing: The crowd that follows a ministry is not a yardstick for measuring God's approval, so the people being carried away by the crowd in a ministry that they had not witnessed in their lifetime (as most of them never saw the old testament prophet) they had no other choice than to conclude that this must be one of the expected prophets to come. Talking about John the Baptist in the same light in John 1:12 "And they asked him, what then? Are thou Elias? And he said I am not. Art thou that prophet? And he answered, No".

When they saw that John the Baptist did not meet up with their guesswork of who the Elijah is, Jesus ministry being the next that followed John the Baptist they thought it wise since John the Baptist have said much about Jesus and they saw the remarkable and miraculous events that followed his ministry they concluded without listening to God as to confirm that he must either be Elijah, Jeremiah or one of the prophets. But Jesus I know is more than these personalities because he is a member of Trinity.

Jesus knowing fully well that the people have an opinion about him, was also interested to know the opinion of his disciples about him since they have been and observed his ministry and he then asked in Matthew 16:15. "He said unto them, But whom say ye that I am?"

Apart from the opinion of others about Jesus, you must have a personal opinion about Jesus because this personal opinion is important and it will determine the level you can work for or follow Jesus. It can determine the level of reverence you will accord him. It will also determine the level of commitment you can put in following him and doing his work.

Jesus needed to know if his followers have a better understanding about him and his ministry an opinion that is not dependent upon the persuasion of men. You as a believer or about to be a believer you must have an opinion about Jesus that will propel you to realize your God given mandate.

The question Jesus asked needed an answer from the disciple as Jesus also needs that answer now from you. Who is this Jesus? Peter responded as in Matthew 16:16. "And Simon Peter answered and said thou art the Christ, the son of the living God".

The answer Peter gave about Jesus was quite correct as attested by Jesus himself. The answer gave us an understanding about the person of Jesus as the son of the living God. It also pointed out to us the ministry and mission of Jesus here on earth as he declared that he is the Christ; which means the savior of mankind.

Because Peter's answer was correct and direct Jesus knew that his knowledge cannot come to a man without the divine revelation. That is the inspiration and answer coming from God and Jesus said in Matthew 16:17. ***"And Jesus answered and said unto him blessed art thou, Simon Bar – Jonah for flesh and blood hath not revealed it unto thee, but my father which is in heaven"***.

Jesus informed us here as he did to Peter that flesh and blood cannot tell who Jesus is and his mission here on earth. It is only a person that is connected to the father that can receive a revelation and understand of who Jesus is.

It then means if you have to know and understand who Jesus is, you must be born again baptized in the Holy Spirit so that you can have access to the Spirit of God that will give you revelation about Jesus.

Whosoever opinion about Jesus you have depended upon in the past and that person is not truly born again and baptized in the Holy Spirit he cannot be competent to give you a proper knowledge about the person and the ministry of Jesus.

Note that this spiritual revelation and understanding brings a person to spirit ordination and elevation. Peter who hitherto was like any of the disciples received divine promotion by virtue of this spiritual revelation. See Matthew 16:18. *"And I say also unto thee that thou art Peter and upon this rock I will build my church and the gates of hell shall not prevail against it"*.

The church needs to go back to the era of divine revelation really coming from God about our Lord Jesus; that will become a tool in the hand of the church against the gates of hell and by so doing the gate of hell shall not prevail against the church.

Who is this Jesus? We may not only depend upon the revelation of Peter as to ascertain who this Jesus is.

The people of Israel did not recognize Jesus as the Messiah apart from those that followed Him or benefited from his ministry. Peter's first confession about who Jesus is came only by revelation. But the second confession came by personal observation as in John 6:68, 69. *"Then Simon Peter answered Him: Lord, to whom shall we go? Thou has the words of eternal life. And we believe and are sure that thou are that Christ, the son of the Living God"*.

By this second confession Peter had tested the first confession and was confident that the first confession about Jesus is real. You can hear Peter saying in the last verse that they are sure that Jesus by his personality is the son of the living God and by his ministry is the Christ.

It requires a lot of testing, passing through experiences with the word of God for you to move from divine revelation to divine reality. Divine revelation is like a foundation upon which you are expected to begin your journey to divine reality. If you start from divine revelation and did not end in divine reality, you have failed in your ministry, and the chances of making heaven are quite remote.

It is not in our interest now to go into what it takes to move from divine revelation to divine revelation to divine reality but I will plead with you never to start the journey from divine revelation without getting divine reality.

There is no other person that knows whether what you preach or confess actually put into practice is real except one that is very close to you either in ministry or in marriage. So Peter being one of the closest person to Jesus, while he was here on earth is really qualified to attest to the fact of whom Jesus is.

John the Apostle who was as close to Jesus as Peter was, has this to write in 1John 5:1. *"Whosoever believeth that Jesus is the Christ is born of God and every one that loveth him that begat loveth him also that is begotten of him"*.

Apart from Apostle Peter and John, there were other witnesses that informed us who Jesus is. Starting from the Almighty God He made a declaration about Jesus and His ministry in Matthew 17:5. *"While he yet spake, behold, a bright cloud overshadowed them; and behold a voice out of the cloud which said, this is my beloved son in whom I am well pleased: hear ye him*". Also in Matthew 3:17.

Jesus also testified about his person as the son of God as in John 10:36. *"Say ye of him, whom the father hath sanctified and sent into the world, thou blasphemest; because I said, I am the son God"*.

Demons also recognized that Jesus is the son of God and that he came for mission here on earth as it is written in Matthew 8:29. *"And behold, they cried out saying what have we to do with thee, Jesus, thou son of God? Art thou come hither to torment us before the time?"* Also in Luke 4:41. *"And devils also came out of many crying out and saying, thou art Christ, the son of God. And He rebuked them and suffered them not to speak: for they knew that He was Christ"*.

We also discovered that Angels were also involved in telling us who this Jesus is and consider Luke 1:32 *"He shall be great, and shall be called the son of the Highest and the Lord God shall give unto him the throne of his father David"*.

There are other testimonies about Jesus from the disciples but one that is quite significant to cloud of witnesses, is the witness of a centurion, whom we may regard as an unbeliever who observed what he said in the course of performing his duty in Matthew 27:54 *"Now when the centurion, and those things that were done they feared greatly saying truly this was the son of God"*.

With this cloud of witnesses we don't need any other prophet to tell us who Jesus is for the Bible said at the mouth of two witnesses a matter is established.

Concerning who Jesus is, we are no longer in doubt about his person and ministry; not only that God the father and his Angels acknowledged who Jesus is but devils and demons also attested to the fact concerning the personality and ministry of our Lord Jesus.

We believe you are not in doubt about who this Jesus is. But remember divine knowledge does not end with divine revelation it shall continue until it gets to divine reality. To help us move from divine revelation about Jesus to divine reality about him we need to consider other issues in bringing out explicitly to us who this Jesus is.

Don't wait until you see the earth quake like the centurion before you believe in the person and ministry of our Lord Jesus but be a believer whose discovery about who Jesus is shall depend upon the scripture and divine revelation supported by divine encounter.

You are welcome!

CHAPTER TWO

THE MANIFESTATION OF JESUS ON EARTH

"AND THE WORD was made flesh and dwelt among us (and we beheld his glory, the glory as of the only begotten of the father) full of grace and truth". – John 1:14.

"And she brought forth her firstborn son, and wrapped him in swaddling clothes and laid him in a manger, because there was no room for them in the inn". – Luke 2:7.

Nobody is in doubt if Jesus actually came to this world because there are various manifestations of Jesus here on earth as recorded in the Bible apart from that there have been various testimonies of people confirming that Jesus is real.

Even in Israel where many of them have not accepted that Jesus is the Christ they still believe and attest to the fact that Jesus came here and walked on the shores of this earth.

Some religious organizations like Islam which though does not accept the Lordship of Jesus also confirms that Jesus is real and was here on earth. The question that comes to mind is in what form did he manifest himself when he came, and what form is he still manifesting himself, or, could it be that since he came and died, his ministry and manifestation ceased?

Jesus we know was here on earth and he manifested his presence in various forms on the earth. The issue of different forms is not to bring confusion or associate him with some satanic manifestation that is contrary to God's standard. From the above-mentioned scripture, we know that Jesus manifested as flesh here on earth.

Jesus as a member of the trinity is a spirit just like God the father and the Holy Spirit. In John 4:24 ***"God is a spirit and they that worship him must worship him in spirit and in truth"***.

In John 6:62 – ***"What and if ye shall see the son of man ascend up where he was before"***. Also in John 10:30 ***"I and my father are one"***. Considering three scriptures quoted above it is obvious Jesus was a spirit as His father was before He was sent to the earth.

There are three ways that Jesus manifested himself and will continue to manifest Himself in those three ways.

Those three ways are:
1) Jesus as the word.
2) Jesus as flesh.
3) Jesus as a spirit.

The first manifestation that Jesus did here on earth was a manifestation as the word of God. In John 1:1 ***"In the beginning was the word, and the word was with God and the word was God"***.

Also in 1John 1:1 ***"that which was from the beginning, which we have heard which we have seen with our eyes, which we have looked upon and our hand have handled, of the word of life"***.

The first manifestation of Jesus here on earth did not start when Jesus was born by Mary. Jesus from the beginning of creation had been there with God. The Bible described him as the word, we take a look at John 1:14 ***"And the word was made flesh and dwelth among us, (and we beheld his glory, the glory as of the only begotten of the father) full of grace and truth"***. This confirms that the word described in John 1:1 refers to no other person than Jesus.

It is also important to note that this "WORD" is not any word but the word of God. It is not a word that proceeded from God the father but this WORD by himself is also God.

The WORD apart from being God has been with God right from the beginning. The WORD did not start manifesting during the New Testament dispensation.

The WORD did not start existing at the beginning of the Old Testament dispensation. The WORD had been in co-self existence with God the father prior to creation. The word was only seen in action when God the father decided to go into creation. The Bible stated in John 1:2, 3 *"The same was in the beginning with God. All things were made by Him; and without Him was not anything made that was made"*.

Considering the scripture above, we discovered that it was not the failure of man that made God to remember the WORD and decided that the WORD should be made manifest. If there may be a time in the past it can be said that God begin to exist, (though it is not possible to state such a time) that was the time the WORD began to exist.

But the first encounter Heaven and earth had with God the father; The WORD was also there to play his own role. In Colossians 1:16 – *"for by him were all things created, that are in earth, visible and invisible, whether they be thrones or dominions or principalities, power: all things were created by Him and he is before all things and by him all things consist"*.

It was the WORD that created everything both in heaven and on earth but it is important to note that verse 17 said it clearly that he existed before all things. That is the WORD had being in existence with God though the earth had not seen his manifestation.

When the time of creation started in Genesis 1:1 when God created the heaven and the earth, the WORD was made manifest for the first time on earth.

But after creation there was a thick darkness upon the earth, God came back through His word to bring light as in Genesis 1:3. The light that came was by the power in the word when God declared it. Looking at John 1:4, 5 "in Him was life, and the life was the light of men. And the light shineth in darkness, and the darkness comprehended it not". The scripture left nobody in doubt that when God said let there be light in the book of Genesis 1:3, the WORD was also involved in that creation.

From that Genesis 1:1 when the WORD first manifested, he did not go on leave or break, he became active in creation. He continued in the creation of light and all the creation that God the father did in Genesis 1:1 – 25.

When it came to creation of man that took over dominion over all God's creatures on earth. God also invited the WORD for the creation of man, in Genesis 1:26 – ***"And God said, let us make man in our own image, after our likeness…*** three plural words were used in the above verse **us**, **our image**, **our likeness** depicts more than one personality bringing in the meaning of Colossians 1:16, it is obvious that the WORD was also involved in the creation of man see also John 1:10, 11. *"He was in the world, and the world was made by him, and the world knew him not. He came unto his own and his own received him not"*.

It is important to note that commandment of God is also the word of God. The commandment of God, also means the law or commandment of God given to Moses on Mount. Sinai is also the word of God produced in a printed form to bring it in a permanent form. This is made available for the people of God to make reference to and have a fulfilled life in walking with God.

The WORD has not ceased to operate after the book of Genesis. The WORD from one generation to another generation has been there giving direction to people how to walk in a way that pleases God the father.

The WORD also manifested through the prophets and priests of God at one time or the other. The priests and prophets of God brought the counsel of God through his word. A typical example is the case of people of Nineveh where Prophet Jonah brought them the word of God which convicted them of their sins and led them to repentance and salvation.

In psalm 107:20 – *"He sent his word, and healed them and delivered them from destructions".*

If we believe this scripture to be true which we must, it then means every healing that took place in the Old Testament dispensation manifested Jesus as the word.

It goes further to mean that every deliverance that took place during the Old Testament dispensation was the word at work.

In 1John 1:1. *"That which was from the beginning, which we have heard, which we have seen with our eyes, which we have looked upon, and our hands have handled, of the word of life".*

Further in John 1:4 – *"In Him was life, and the life was the light of men".* The first scripture above informs us that this is not just any word but it is the WORD that has life in it. That is why it is the word of life. Also in John 1:4, we recognized that life is in the word so that every situation that has contact with the word no matter how dead the situation may be must receive life. In Ezekiel 37:5 – *"Thus saith the Lord God unto these bones, Behold, I will cause breath to enter into you, and ye shall live".*

Here the WORD of God had encounter with the dry bones in the midst of the valley, despite the deadness and the impossibility (in the eyes of men) for the situation to be restored, when the word of God came through his Prophet Ezekiel, the dry bones received life in the WORD and lived.

The miracles we read that Jesus did when he was on earth started during the Old Testament. All the miracles that the prophets did using the word of God and by *"thus say the Lord"* are miracles performed by the WORD. Jesus was still manifesting his presence in such miracles. To give credence to the above assertion let us look at 1 Corinthians 10:4 – *"and did all drink the same spiritual drink, for they drank of that spiritual Rock that followed them: and that Rock was Christ".* Psalm 78:15 – *"He clave the rocks in the wilderness and gave them drink as out of the great depths".* The two scriptures referred to the incident that took place in Exodus 17:6 – *"Behold, I will stand before thee there upon the rock in Horeb; and thou shalt smite the rock, and there shall come out of it that the people may drink. And Moses did so in the sight of the elders of Israel".*

In the book of Exodus 17:6 no reference was made to the WORD being involved in the miracle but it was in 1Corinthains 10:4 that a deep revelation came out of that incidence that the rock that brought out water was Jesus.

Perhaps that may be the reason God was annoyed with Moses in the sense that God told him to talk to the rock instead he smote the rock as was recorded in the book of Numbers 20:11, 12 – *"And Moses lifted up his hand, and with his rod he smote the rock twice: and the water came out abundantly. And the congregation drank, and their beast also. And the LORD spake unto Moses and Aaron, because ye believed me not, to sanctify me in the eyes of the children of Israel, therefore ye shall not bring this congregation into the land which I have given them".*

Jesus as the WORD did not manifest in the creation or other miracles mentioned and went to rest rather he was still active manifesting himself in different ways. In Colossians 1:17 – *"and he is before all things, and by him all things consist"*. Also in Hebrews 1:3 – *"who being the brightness of his glory, and the express image of his person, and upholding all things by the word of his power…"*

By his word of power all things are upheld and sustained eternally. The word was from Genesis chapter 1 to Malachi Chapter4:6. The word held all things together and kept manifesting in different form not just creating things but also in charge over created things.

The second manifestation of Jesus was when he came to the earth in flesh. This manifestation through flesh took place at the beginning of the New Testament era.

In Matthew 1:21, 25 – *"And she shall bring forth a son, and thou shalt call his name JESUS: for he shall save his people from their sins… and knew her not till she had brought forth her first born son: and he called his name JESUS"*.

In Luke 2:7 – *"And she brought forth her firstborn son, and wrapped him in swaddling clothes, and laid him in a manger, because there was no room for them in the inn"*.
John 1:14 – *"and the word was made flesh and dwelt among us, (and we beheld his glory, the glory as of the only begotten of the father) full of grace and truth"*.

The scriptures above give us an understanding that Jesus indeed came to this world in the form of man. It has been stated that the Old Testament began with man made in the image of God (Gen. 1:26) while the New Testament began with God manifesting in the image of man (John 1:14).

It further informed us why that which happened in the Old Testament which defeated God's purpose came back in New Testament to actualize God's purpose. The man made in the image of God was defeated by Satan in the Garden Of Eden (Gen. 2:8) but the God made in the image of man defeated Satan at the cross of Calvary (Col. 2:15).

It is not in doubt that Jesus came here on earth; even the Israelites who doubted his messiah ship never doubted he came here on earth.

We may not have seen him physically but evidence abound that he came in the flesh. Some people that saw him physically testified to that, see I John1:1 – 3 *"that which was from the beginning which we have heard, which we have seen with our eyes, which we have looked upon, and our hands have handled, of the word of life. (for the life was manifested and we have seen it, and bear witness, and show unto you that eternal life, which was with the father and was manifested unto us) that which we have seen and heard declare we unto you, that ye also may have fellowship with us: and truly our is with the father, and with his son Jesus Christ".*

The manifestation of Jesus in the flesh came by way of prophecy when Jesus was still manifesting as the word in the Old Testament as in Isaiah 7:14 – *"Therefore the Lord himself shall give you a sign, Behold a virgin shall conceive and bear a son, and shall call his name Immanuel".*

In Zachariah 9:9 – *"Rejoice greatly O daughter of Zion, shout, O daughter of Jerusalem: behold, thy king cometh unto thee: he is just, and having salvation lowly, and riding upon an ass, and upon a colt the foal of an ass".*

Even in the New Testament before Jesus manifested in the flesh; the vessel God prepared to use was also informed about it by angel Gabriel in Luke 1:31 – *"And behold thou shalt conceive in thy womb, and bring forth a son, and shalt call his name JESUS".*

Joseph the husband of Mary who did not understand how Mary became pregnant without meeting with him also received a visitation in the dream by the Angel of God in Matthew 1:21, 23 – *"And she shall bring forth a son, and thou shalt call his name JESUS: for he shall save his people from their sins. Behold, a virgin shall be with child and shall bring a son and they shall call his name Immanuel which being interpreted is God with us".*

Finally when Jesus came in the flesh, the Angel of God came to announce his birth unto the world: to the shepherds in Luke 2:10, 11. *"And the angel said unto them, fear not; for, behold, I bring you good tidings of great Joy, which shall be to all people. For unto you is born this day in the city of David a Saviour, which is Christ the Lord".*

The third manifestation of Jesus here on earth was a manifestation as Spirit. Jesus who manifested in the flesh died on the cross for our sins but it did not end there because that same Jesus resurrected from the death and appeared unto so many people. From that time till the second coming of Jesus, he will continue to manifest in the spirit in John 20:9 *"for as yet they knew not the scripture, that he must rise again from the dead".*

In Mark 16:6 – *"And he saith unto them, be not affrighted: ye seek Jesus of Nazareth, which was crucified: he is risen, he is not here behold the place where they laid him".*

The ministry of Jesus did not end in the grave, Jesus resurrected from the grave not just from the grave but from Hell. Jesus resurrection was not done in secrecy but there are biblical and empirical proofs of the resurrection of Jesus.

After Jesus resurrected he did not sneak into Heaven and said Goodbye to the earth. He manifested as a spirit several ways. Though Jesus had a body and all that makes a body even the mark of the nails upon his body were there after the resurrection. His resurrection is not like somebody that died and rose up from the dead like Lazarus and Jairus daughter.

Those people retained their mortal bodies and did everything according to the laws of carnality but in the case of Jesus his own was more than rising from the dead. He resurrected with an immortal body that had a spiritual manifestation that made him to operate according to the law that govern immortality in John 20:19 – 20 – *"Then the same day at evening being the first day of the week, when the doors were shut where the disciples were assembled for fear of the Jews, came Jesus and stood in the midst and saith unto them, peace be unto you. And when he had so said, he showed unto them his hands and his side. Then were the disciples glad, when they saw the Lord"*.

Also in Acts 1:3 – *"to whom also he showed himself alive after his passion by many infallible proofs being seen of them forty days, and speaking of the things pertaining to the kingdom of God"*.

There are numerous appearances of Jesus as spirit or a personality with immortal body. The first appearance was to Mary Magdalene as she remained at the site of the tomb after Peter and John had left. In Mark 16:9 – *"Now when Jesus was risen early the first day of the week, he appeared first to Mary Magdalene out of whom he had cast seven devils"*.

Jesus also manifested to the head of his apostles Peter in Luke 24:34 – *""saying the Lord is risen indeed and hath appeared to Simon.*

Jesus manifested to two disciples as in Mark 16:12, 13. He also manifested to the ten disciples as in Luke 24:36 – 43. He manifested to the eleven disciples when Thomas was present as in John 20:26 – ***"And after eight days again his disciples were within, and Thomas with them, then came Jesus, the Doors being shut stood in the midst, and said, peace be unto you"***.

Before Jesus ascension into heaven he appeared at Mount Olives before the presence of the eleven disciples. The purpose of this appearance was for the eleven disciples to witness his ascension into heaven. God does not do anything in secrecy. He must leave a witness, see Acts 1:3 – 9. This appearance is also important because it became an avenue for the Angel of God to announce to the disciples of the second coming of Jesus.

The manifestation of Jesus as spirit or personality with immortal body did not stop at the day of ascension of Jesus. This manifestation has continued in the lives of other disciples as recorded in the bible.

The first manifestation after ascension was unto Stephen see Act 7:55 – "But the, being full of the Holy Ghost, looked up steadfastly into heaven, and saw the glory of God, and Jesus standing on the right hand of God". There are many mysteries shrouded in this passage which may be unveiled in other books.

Paul also had an experience with Jesus when he manifested in the spirit as in Act 9:3 – 6 with emphasis on verse 5 – "***And the Lord said, I am Jesus whom thou persecutes: it is hard for thee to kick against the pricks"***. Apart from this first experience Paul had, John also had the same encounter at the beginning of the book of Revelation 1:1 – 20 with emphasis on verse 1, 17, 18 – ***"And the Revelation of Jesus Christ, which God gave unto him to show unto his servants things which must shortly come to pass, and he sent and signified it by his angel unto his servant John… And when I saw him, I fell at his feet as dead. And he laid his right hand upon me saying unto me, fear not; I am the first and the*** *last. I am he that liveth, and was dead; and behold I am alive for evermore Amen; and have the keys of hell and of death".*

This form of manifestation has not ended, it will continue until the second coming of Jesus. We too have had this type of experience in different forms, sometimes it is through dream, vision or trance. Note that in your dream, when you have an attack from spiritual forces the moment you mention Jesus or the blood of Jesus, that spiritual forces is defeated. That is the continuation of the manifestation of Jesus as Spirit in our lives. He promised he will not leave us; he is with us till the end of the world or the end of our lives here on earth. Matthew 28:20 – *"teaching them to observe all things whatsoever I have commanded you: and lo I am with you always, even unto the end of the world. Amen".*

CHAPTER THREE

WHAT HAS HE COME TO DO?

The God we serve is a God of purpose. For everything God does, He does for a particular reason either to please Himself or to please His children.

It is established in our mind that Jesus came here on earth not on his own accord but because God the father sent him to come. In John 4:34 – ***"Jesus saith unto them, my meat is to do the will of Him that sent me, and to finish His work".***

Jesus was sent by God the father but His coming to the earth is to fulfill God's purpose here on earth. Ephesians 3:11 – ***"according to the eternal purpose which he purposed in Christ Jesus our Lord".***

Jesus came for a purpose, to do a lot both for God's purpose and for humanity purpose. This book is not enough to enumerate all that Jesus came to do but we are going to limit it to some points and our believe is that the Holy Spirit who will guide us unto all truth will expatiate them for us.

(1) The invisible God

One of the purposes for which Jesus came was to reveal to us the invisible God. In John 1:18 – ***"No man hath seen God at any time; the only begotten which is in the bosom of the Father, he hath declared him".***
It is obvious that no one has ever seen God right from creation till the time Jesus was born.

There were men in the past that had wonderful time and deep relationship with God but never saw the face of God. Let us consider first of all Moses.

Moses had a tremendous close relationship with God. He never saw the face of God as to tell us how God looks like, it was not his ministry to bring to our understanding how God looks like. Though he never desired it but only asked to know the way of the Lord.

We read in Exodus 33:11 – *"And the Lord spake unto Moses face to face as a man speaketh unto his friend…"* Looking at this verse in isolation to other verses of the chapter one may conclude that Moses saw the face of God. But as we read the other verses we discovered that he never saw the face of God in Exodus 33:20, 22, 23. – *"And he said, thou canst not see my face: for there shall no man see me and live… and it shall come to pass, while my glory passeth by, that I will put thee in a cleft of the rock, and will cover thee with my hand while I pass by and I will take away mine hand, and thou shalt see my back parts, but my face shall not be seen".*

Moses did not see the face of God but he only asked God so that he will know the way of the Lord, in Exodus 33:13 – *"Now therefore, I pray thee, if I have found grace in thy sight, show me now thy way, that I may know thee…"* Moses request was granted and God gave him the opportunity to become the law giver not only the ten commandments but other laws. The best way to know God's way is through his laws just like the Bible.

Another man that had great encounter with God was Elijah but it is still on record that Elijah never saw God, he only heard the word of God as in 1Kings 19:9 – *"And he came hither unto a cave, and lodged there, and behold the word of the Lord came to him and he said unto him, what does thou here, Elijah?"* Elijah did not see but the only thing he was qualified to receive was the word of God (I believe it may not be out of place to say it was the manifestation of Jesus).

Jesus is the only person that has seen God and knows how God looks. Though Genesis 1:26 told us that we were made in the image and likeness of God but we know it is not sufficient point to say that we all have God's resemblance. But Jesus knows God's resemblance and look and has come to reveal to us his invisible nature and making it visible but with a warning still not to make any image in anything either in heaven or the earth. So Jesus came to reveal the invisible God to us see John 14:9 – *"Jesus saith unto him, have I been so long time with you? And yet hast thou not known me, Philip? He that hath seen me hath seen the father; and how sayest thou then, show us the father?"*

(2) <u>To Fulfill Prophesy</u>

Another reason why Jesus came was to fulfill prophecy given by the prophets in old time and also to fulfill God's word to humanity though man fell from the grace of God but God did not leave man to perish, God made provision for the redemption of mankind.

Though God tried to use the law as a way of bringing redemption to mankind nevertheless he made provision for a better way to bring the fulfillment of this redemption.

The fulfillment of God's first prophecy of Jesus coming to do a work for Him in the redemption of mankind was immediately after the fall of man in Genesis 3:15 – *"and I will put enmity between thee and the woman and between thy seed and her seed, it shall bruise thy head and thou shalt bruise his heel"*.

This was a direct word of God to the serpent which the devil used in bringing about the fall of man. God declared a war against the devil which depended on the seed of a woman to undo what the devil had done to mankind.

This explains why Jesus must come as a seed of a woman (Mary) Luke 2:7 – *"And she brought forth her born son, and wrapped him in swaddling clothes and laid him in a manger, because there was no room for them in the inn".*

Apart from being the seed of a woman, Jesus had a mandate to deal with the devil as to undo what the devil did to mankind in Colossians 2:15 – *"And having spoiled principalities and powers. He made a show of them openly triumphing over them in it".*

Jesus went to the cross and by going to the cross he set mankind free from the captivity of the devil. Not only setting man free from devil's bondage, he equally gave man the power and authority to keep the devil at bay as in Luke 10:19 – *"Behold I give unto you power to trend on serpents and scorpions and over all the power of the enemy, and nothing shall by any means hurt you".*

Jesus is telling mankind that he has given him the power to overcome the devil even if he manifests like a serpent as he did in the Garden of Eden, we should be able to tread upon it without receiving a devastating attack from the devil. Remember when we fail to use the power given to us by Jesus to tread upon serpent; the serpent may exercise the power to bruise our heel. Jesus has come to fulfill his prophecy and remind us that the war between the devil, its manifestations, agents and mankind is still on 1Peter 5:8 – *"Be sober, be vigilant: Because your adversary the devil, as a roaring Lion, walketh about, seeking whom he may devour".*

(3) <u>**To Make A Sacrifice For Our Sins.**</u>
In 1John 3:5 – *"And ye know that he was manifested to take away our sins, and in him is no sin".* Jesus came to be sacrifice for our sins. When Adam sinned, sin entered into the world in Romans 5:12 – *"Wherefore, as by one man sin entered into the world, and death by sin; and so death passed upon all men, for that all have sinned".*

By the meaning of the above verse all mankind also sinned as a consequence of Adam's sin. No man born into this world can escape this sin that followed generations after Adam. Any person born into this world was born in sin even though your parents are ministers of God you are born in sin and you must have a need for redemption in Psalms 51:5 – *"Behold, I was shapen in iniquity and in sin did my mother conceive me".* Further in Romans 3:23 – *"For all has sinned, and come short of the glory of God".*

When sin entered into the world God made an effort through the laws to bring the required righteousness that will bring redemption to mankind. These laws came with different offerings like burnt offering, peace offering and sin offering. In these offerings animal sacrifice was required by God to bring a purging of the sin of the people. Despite the number of animals killed it was not satisfactory to God to bring a permanent redemption to mankind: the animal blood only covered their sins but did not blot them out.

In Hebrew 10:4-6, 10, 12 – *"For it is not possible that the blood of bulls and of goats should takeaway sins. Wherefore, when he cometh into the world, he saith sacrifice and offering thou wouldest not but a body hast thou prepared me, in burnt offerings and sacrifices for sin thou hast had no pleasure. By the which will we are sanctified through the offering of the body of Jesus Christ once for all.---- but this man, after he had offered one sacrifice for sins forever, sat down on the right hand of God.*

We know that Jesus who came as a sacrifice for our sins did not come for only one man, a race, a particular religion but for every mankind. Hebrew 2:9. It is only the people that are willing to accept Jesus sacrifice for our sins that will benefit from it. Hebrew 2:9 – *"But we see Jesus, who was made a little lower than the angels for the suffering of death crowned with glory and honour that he by the grace of God should taste death for every man".*

(4) <u>To Reconcile Man To God</u>

Another purpose for which Jesus came into the world was to reconcile man back to God. When we talk about reconciliation, it then means that a relationship hitherto had existed between two parties. Secondly the relationship had broken down and thirdly; there is a desire by one of the parties or all the parties to be reconciled.

When God created mankind God was happy in Genesis 1:36 – *"And God saw everything that he had made and behold it was very good..."* Thereafter God established a relationship between Him and man. This relationship resulted in a fellowship that made God come in a cool of the day to have fellowship with man. But in this particular fellowship with man, God discovered that man had willfully broken the fellowship and consequently broken the relationship with God thereby lost the glory of God, Romans 3:23 – ***"All have sinned, and come short of the glory of God".***

God cherished the relationship he had with mankind and made several attempts to bring in a reconciliation in Isaiah 1:18 – ***"Come and let us reason together saith the Lord: though your sins be as scarlet, they shall be as white as snow, though they be red like crimson, they shall be as wool".***

Mankind did not respond to the call of God, still God chose to come by himself through His son Jesus to bring back this reconciliation. In 2Crointhians 5:19 – ***"To with, that God was in Christ, reconciling the world unto himself, not imputing their trespasses unto them and hath committed unto us the word of reconciliation".***

God so desirous to have us back to him after we had offended him, employ the services of our Lord Jesus to come into the issue to bring reconciliation between man and God in 1Timothy 2:5,6 – ***"For there is one God and one mediator between God and men, the man Christ Jesus who gave himself a ransom for all, to be testified in due time".***

(5) <u>To Be The Priest Needed</u>

What broke the relationship between God and man was as a result of sin. This sin was of general application, no man born of any woman was exempted from this sin and the consequences of sin.

As illustrated above, God was quite desirous to reconcile man back to Himself but he needed a sacrificial lamb that will become a propitiation for the sin of the people and remain in that position as a priest doing a function on behalf of God to the people and on behalf of the people to God. For God to have a priest that is sinless and have the power to stand as an atonement for the sin of the people and remain a priest thereafter, none was found worthy to satisfy that before and after Jesus sacrifice. See the book of Revelation 5:4 – *"And I wept much because no man was found worthy to open and to read the book, neither to look thereon"*.

Jesus was the only qualified candidate. But if he must function effectively he must come to the earth and possess flesh and blood, he must be tempted in the world and have an adequate experience of what is obtainable here on earth so that he can effectively feel how the people of the world feel and be in a better position to sympathize and understand their trials, suffering, afflictions and temptations as in Hebrews 4:15 – *"For we have not a high priest which cannot be touched with the feeling of our infirmities; but was in all points tempted like as we are, yet without sin"*.

So when Jesus came, he became our high priest both for sacrifice for sins and to maintain a continued relationship with God by walking with God. Jesus became the much need high Priest God required in Hebrews 2:17 – *"Wherefore in all things it behooved him to be made like unto his brethren that he might be a merciful high priest in things pertaining to God, to make reconciliation for the sins of the people".*

(6) <u>To Destroy The Devil And His Works.</u>

The man made in the image of God was defeated and made a captive by the devil in the Garden of Eden as recorded in the Old Testament but in the New Testament, God that came in the image of man defeated the same devil and set men at liberty from the captivity of the devil.

In Hebrews 2:14 – *"For as much then as the children are partakers of flesh and blood, he also himself likewise took part of the same, that through death he might destroy him that had the power of death, that is the devil".*

The reason why men succumb to men of underworld is that they consider them having power of death by virtue of the instrument of destruction they have at their disposal. Similarly men have surrendered their cars keys and handed over large sums of money to the men of the underworld for the same reason. So it is with man, the moment man fell through sin, they became subject to the devil that by reason of sin the devil has power of death over them as the scripture puts it that death entered into the word through sin.

All men came in subjection to the devil so simply demand of their life, money, marriage or business by the devil with little threat men gives over whatever it is to the devil because sin and fall of man gave him power over death. So any little threat of death over man, he will quickly surrender to devil. Thanks be to God for Jesus that came and saw the state of man this moved Jesus to tears in the case of Lazarus, a righteous child of God.

Jesus knew that he was going to heal Lazarus as recorded in the book of John chapter 11 but when he came to the tomb the bible recorded, *"Jesus wept"*. The question is why should Jesus weep when he knew he was going to raise Lazarus from death? But Jesus understanding the helpless condition of man knew that whether he was righteous or not he was still subject to this helpless condition of the power of death, as the bible puts it, "if the foundation is destroyed what can the righteous do".

But thank God that Jesus came and destroyed the devil who had the power over death and collected the keys of hell and death as recorded in Revelation 1:18 – *"I am he that liveth, and was dead and behold, I am alive for evermore Amen; and have the keys of hell and of death"*.

When man fell and became subject to captivity of the devil, the devil began to introduce his own programs, reasoning, system and world view. The Enemy evolved a world system to suit the fallen nature of man. The fallen man has no choice but to accept and help to promote Enemy's agenda and made man's world to lieth in wickedness as it recorded in 1John 5:19 – *"And we know that we are of God and the whole world lieth in wickedness"*.

We may not enumerate all the works of the devil because they are many but the good news is that when Jesus came he not only destroyed the devil, he also destroyed the works of the devil. See 1John 3:8 – ***"He that committed sin is of the devil, for the devil sinneth from the beginning for this purpose the son of God was manifested, that he might destroy the works of the devil"***.

(7) <u>**To Deliver Men From Fear Of Death**</u>
Hebrews 2:15 –***"And deliver them, who through fear of death were all their lifetime subject to bondage"***.

It is true that the devil had power over death but this came as a result of man's fall from the commandment of God and the consequences of this fall as pronounced by God is death.

In Romans 6:23 – ***"For all the wages of sin is death, but the gift of God is eternal life through Jesus Christ our Lord"***. Also in Genesis 2:16, 17 – ***"And the Lord God commanded the man saying of every tree of the garden thou mayest freely eat: but of the tree of the knowledge of good and evil, thou shalt not eat of it: for in the day that thou eatest thereof thou shalt surely die"***.

By above pronouncement by God, when man sinned, he became subject to the power of death which gave the devil power of death over man.

Consequently fear of death came into man. The fear of death also became a snare to man. Man can do anything in order to secure his life to the extent that evil men have to enter into covenant with death. In Isaiah 28:18 – ***"And your covenant with death shall be disannulled, and your agreement with hell shall not stand, when the over flowing scourge shall pass through, then ye shall be trodden down by it"***.

But when Jesus came the people of Israel only knew him as a miracle worker who could only heal but not raise the dead. In John chapter 11, His people, including Mary and Martha were telling Jesus that if he was there earlier Lazarus would not have died. But Jesus introduced himself as life and resurrection. After Jesus raised Lazarus from the dead there was also another conspiracy to kill Jesus and Lazarus. But you know at this point in time Lazarus had been delivered from the fear of death. Since the advent of Jesus and till today, believers are no more afraid of death as they now see death as only a means of transition to heaven.

(8) <u>He Came To Save The Lost</u>
Mathew 18:11 – *"For the son of man is come to save that which was lost"*.

Jesus actually came to save those that are lost. We know that the fall of Adam was a fall for everyone. In Isaiah 53:6 – *"All we like sheep have gone astray; we have turned every one to his own way; and Lord hath laid on him the iniquity of us all"*.

One of the consequences of the fall of man is that man lost his relationship and fellowship with God. Man was driven out of the Garden of Eden and the usual fellowship God did have with Adam at the cool of the day was broken. That lost relationship and fellowship became the portion of man. Secondly there was no guarantee for man to be in heaven. The possibility of another going to meet the Lord in heaven was no longer there.

In Colossians 1:21 we read – *"And you, that were some time alienated and enemies in your mind by wicked works, yet now hath he reconciled"*.

The main reason why Jesus came and died for us was to save us from our lost position of broken fellowship and relationship with God.

(9) <u>To Provide an Example for Believers</u>
In Romans 1:19 – *"Because that which may be known of God is manifest in them, for God hath showed it unto them"*. Though man came short of the glory of God when he sinned against him, God still gave him another opportunity to know that he exist and if they should repent and seek him, they will find him. But man in his fallen status could not desire to know and serve God he would rather choose the path that pleases his lust rather than God. In Romans 1:20 – *"For the invisible things of him from the creation of the world are clearly seen, being understood by the things that are made, even his eternal power and Godhead; so that they are without excuse"*. Man would rather choose to ignore God and lean on his own understanding which resulted in his wild behavior. Romans 1:28 – 32 – *"And even as they did not like to retain God in their knowledge, God gave them over to a reprobate mind, to do those things which are not convenient, being filled with all unrighteousness, fornication, wickedness, covetousness, maliciousness, full of envy, murder, debate, deceit, malignity, whispers, backbiters, haters of God, despiteful, proud, boasters, inventors of evil things, disobedient to parent, without understanding, covenant breakers, without natural affection, implacable, unmerciful: who knowing the judgment of God that they which*

commit such things are worthy of death, not only do the same, but have pleasure in them that do them".

Even though Jesus came to save us there is need for us to consciously change our way of life which we need to do after we are born again. He needed to show us by example how to live our lives to conform to the acceptable standard of God. In 1Peter 2:21 – *"For even hereunto were ye called: because Christ also suffered for us, leaving us an example, that ye should follow his steps".*

Jesus came to show us the way of life, how we should follow it and what is expected of us as it is stated in 1John 2:6 – *"He that saith he abideth in him ought himself also so to walk even as he walketh".*

(10)   <u>To Heal the Broken hearted</u>

Jesus came to heal those who are physically and spiritually sick. Unfortunately the world could only see him healing those who are physically sick. But Jesus came and moved beyond raising the dead. He also came to touch those whose heart were broken and needed healing.

Jesus also came for those who are emotionally sick. Perhaps your heart is broken because of a contract you are pursuing did not succeed, or the employment somebody promised you failed. Perhaps marriage proposal did not work out even after you have put in much to make it succeed, it may be that you have been married for several years and there are no fruits of the womb to bless the home and there are frustrations here and there, something coming from mother in-law and sister in-laws or sometimes from your husband, colleagues or neighbours and as a result of that your heart is broken. Perhaps you may be at a cross road because your landlord is on your neck, the children's school fees are there to settle and perhaps your car has problems that require huge sums of money and there are financial needs from your parents and home and because of these your heart is broken. Hear the word as it is written in Luke 4:18 – *"The spirit of the Lord is upon me because he hath anointed me to preach the gospel to the poor. He hath sent me to heal the broken hearted…"*

It could be you lost a dear friend, husband, wife, parents, son or daughter and as a result your heart is broken. Don't worry, Jesus came to heal that broken hearted. In Luke 7:11 – 15 we read *"And it came to pass the day after that he went into a city called Nain and many of his disciples went with him and much people. Now when he came nigh to the gate of the city, behold, there was a dead man carried out, the only son of his mother, and she was a widow: and much people of the city was with her. And when the Lord saw her, he had compassion on her, and said unto her weep not. And he came and touched the bier and they that bare him stood still. And he that was dead sat up and began to speak. And he delivered him to his mother".*

(11)   <u>To Give Life – Abundant Life</u>
John 10:10 – *"The thief cometh not, but for to steal, and to kill, and to destroy: I am come that they might have life and that they might have it more abundantly".*

The devil is the thief, who started from the Garden of Eden to steal and he is still in the business of stealing. The devil stole eternal life from Adam and stole the fellowship that brought God and Adam together.

The devil as the thief has not stopped stealing, killing and destroying. The devil has been going about stealing health from people and when Jesus came, he gave them life that brought healing. The thief killed Lazarus and Jesus came and gave life. The thief also came with the purpose of destroying the faith and life of Peter; thank God Jesus was available to give life to Peter's faith and also gave him real life.

What is it that the devil has stolen from you? It may be your car, through accident or loan, it may be your wife or husband, it could be your health. Jesus said I have come that **You** (that is reading this book) may have life: not just to have life but to have life in abundance.

But you can't have this abundant life except you accept Jesus into your life. It is true that he came to give life but you must as a matter of fact accept him into your life.

In John 3:36 – ***"He that believeth on the son hath everlasting life and he that believeth not the son shall not see life, but the wrath of God abideth on him"***.

So if you need life and life that is in abundance, you have a role to play and that role is that you must accept him into your life. Jesus said in Revelation 3:20 – ***"Behold, I stand at the door, and knock: if any man hear my voice, and open the door, I will come in to him, and I will sup with him, and he with me"***.

(12) <u>To Glorify The Father</u>
In John 14:13 – *"And whatsoever ye shall ask in my name, that will I do that the father may be glorified in the son"*.

In the Garden of Eden when man sinned, the bible recorded that man fell short of the glory of God. God could no longer manifest his glory through man.

Any event that brings out the glory of God is no longer a normal event rather a supernatural event. Sometimes God creates this situation or allows the situation so that people can see His glory. In John 9:1 – 3 – *"And as Jesus passed by, he saw a man which was blind from his birth. And his disciples asked him, saying, Master, who did sin, this man, or his parents, that he was born blind? Jesus answered, neither hath this man sinned nor his parents: but that the works of God should be made manifest in him"*.

Today, through Jesus we have known God the father as the King of Glory.

CHAPTER FOUR

IS IT NECESSARY THAT JESUS SHOULD COME?

(1) The Laws Were Not Adequate

The Bible tells us that God created the heavens and earth at the beginning. After this, God created man in his own image as in Genesis 1:26 – 28. Because of God's love for mankind He created, He also prepared a Garden called Garden of Eden and put all that man needs for existence into it and placed man in this beautiful Garden to dress it and keep it.

Thereafter the enemy of our soul the devil who felt jealous of the level of trust God committed into the hand of man plotted against man as to wrestle the power and the glory from him. The devil only succeeded in collecting the power but never the glory.

When man fell God though felt disappointed but it never took God unawares. The bible said before the foundation of the world Jesus had been chosen by God to redeem mankind. It then means the All Knowing God knew that which befell man before it happened.

After man failed, did God cross his hand and say to hell with man, or did God think of wiping away all mankind from the surface of the earth and replacing them with another set of beings – though we know that he Has the power to do it but He did not do so. Rather God began a journey to reconcile man back to Himself without compromising His standard of holiness and righteousness.

The first thing God did was to introduce God's command known as God's statutes, commandments or laws. These set of rules to govern man's relationship with God and man's relationship with his fellow man was now known as the laws of God.

God introduced his laws into the affairs of man so as to establish the righteousness required for man to be reconciled to him.

The question now is to what extent have these laws achieved the desires of God? One cannot say that the laws of God failed totally. It succeeded to the extent that men who were able to hearken to the laws of God excelled and God used them to magnify Himself.

It is these same laws that made Jesus to come, the reason being that some things were not profitable from the laws so that the whole race in the world can appropriate its purpose and benefit from it.

What are these things that made the laws not adequate as to necessitate the coming of our Lord Jesus?

(a)   The basic thing the law was meant to achieve was to bring salvation to the entire people but the law could not accomplish this.

(b)

All who seek salvation by the works of the law are under the curse, because it is impossible for them to keep the law and come up to its standards. The law pronounced all cursed who would not continue "in all things that are written in the book of the law to do them."

In James 2:10 we read– *"For whosoever shall keep the whole law, and yet offend in one point, he is guilty of all…"*

In Galatians 3:11 we read – *"But that no man is justified by the law in the sight of God, it is evident: for, the just shall live by faith".*

The law was made to be good because it came as a result of sin Romans 7:12 – *"Wherefore the law is holy and the commandment holy and just and good".* See also Galatians 3:19 – *"Wherefore then serveth the law? It was added because of transgressions, till the seed should come to whom the promise was made; and it was ordained by Angels the hand of a mediator."*

Despite the fact that the law was added because of sin and the law was good and holy, there were certain things the law could not achieve for mankind such as

    (i)   Justify – see Romans 3:20 – *"Therefore by the deeds of the law there shall no flesh be justified in his sight: for by the law is the knowledge of sin".*

    (ii)   Make perfect – in Hebrew 7:19 – *"for the law made nothing perfect, but the bringing in of a better hope did, by the which we draw nigh unto God".*

    (iii)   Free from sin and death.

    (iv)   Free from condemnation

    (v)   Give freedom.

    (vi)   Give inheritance.

    (vii)   Bring righteousness

    (viii)   Impart Holy Spirit.

    (ix)   Perform miracles.

    (x)   Free from the curse

    (xi)   Impart faith.

(xii)   Impart Grace
(xiii) Control sin in man
(xiv)   Keep man from sin
(xv)   Enable man to obey.

This was the purpose of doing away with the law which also brought enmity and made the middle wall of partition between Jews and Gentiles. God planned to make both classes one new man; the church, so making peace between all men.

The law as we have seen is not only good but holy but despite that, it could not achieve God's purpose to reconcile man back to Him and this necessitated the coming of our Jesus to accomplish the purpose of God for mankind see Galatians 2:16 – ***"Knowing that a man is not justified by the works of the law, but by faith of Jesus Christ, that we might be justified by the faith of Christ, and not by the works of the law shall no flesh be justified."***

Also in Romans 8:3–4, - ***"For what the law could not do in that it was weak through the flesh, God sending his own son in the likeness of sinful flesh and for sin, condemned sin in the flesh: that the righteousness of the law might be fulfilled in us, who walk not after the flesh but after the spirit."***

The law's weakness to accomplish its purpose made it necessary that Jesus must come to do that which the law could not do so if you are still depending upon the law for justification and redemption. Know that you cannot achieve that unless you humble yourself and commit your life into the hands of Jesus who is able to bring redemption and justification. Though when Jesus came, He did not come to out rightly condemn the laws but to fulfill the laws that are still relevant to our Christian life and encourage us to still practice them, e.g. payment of tithe etc.

(2) <u>THE SACRIFICE OF BULLS AND GOATS WAS NO LONGER SATISFACTORY</u>

In Hebrews 10:1 – *"For the law having a shadow of good things to come, and not the very image of the things, can never with those sacrifices, which they offered year by year continually, make the comers thereunto perfect."*

There were a lot of sacrifices required during the dispensation of the law by the priest of God.

These sacrifices were done every year as to purge the sins of the people as to meet with the righteous demand of God. In Hebrews 10:2-3 – *"for then would they not have ceased to be offered? because that the worshippers once purged should have had no more conscience of sins. But in those sacrifices there is a remembrance again made of sins every year."*

Despite the repetition of these sacrifices of bulls and goats they could not achieve the desired goal.

In Hebrews 10:4 – *"for it is not possible that the blood of bulls and of goats should take away sins."*

It does not mean that the Old Testament sacrifices were irrelevant or ineffective, but the issue is that these sacrifices were only meant to appease God as to escape punishment from the sins committed. Sometimes you see a man who commit sin and will ask for mercy perhaps bring animal sacrifice for sin though God will forgive the person but the person will still experience the consequences of that sin. David is an example of a man whose sins were forgiven by God but he experienced the consequences of his sins.

So the sacrifices of bulls and goats through burnt sacrifice, sin offering, peace offering etc could not remove sin and does not have the ability of removing the consequences that follow the sin. This could happen to an individual, a family or a nation. The nation of Israel suffered it when they murmured against God, though He forgave them when Moses interceded, but the consequence of the sin was still invoked and that is the visitation of fiery serpent upon the people of Israel which led to death of some of them.

We were made to understand in Hebrews 10:6 that – *"in burnt offerings and sacrifices for sin, thou hast had no pleasure."*

That these offerings and sacrifices does not satisfy God again. He has no pleasure in them. The reason being that when you keep on doing one thing every time it will certainly loose its value or worth and taste. God is a God of variety in righteousness. Variety is the spice of life they say, moreover the required standard needed to make the offerings and sacrifices acceptable were no longer there. The people could no longer maintain the righteous standard required to make it a sweet smelling savour unto God as Noah did in the bible Genesis 8:20 – 21, - *"And Naoh builded an altar unto the Lord and took of every clean beast, and of every clean fowl, and offered burnt offerings on the altar. And the Lord smelled a sweet savor, and the Lord said in his heart…"*

If then God is no longer having pleasure in our sacrifices of bull and goats, the hope of salvation unto man is gone; the hope of redemption is forgotten and the hope of restoration becomes a mirage. Then what should be done as to bring man out of this problem? God is willing to see man liberated but man could not fulfill the standard needed to make the structures on ground work as a result, the restoration of man's relationship with God became thinner and thinner until it became almost impossible to see righteous ones working with God.

But thank God that before the foundation of the world Jesus had taken up the appointment of redemption of man and was prepared to pay the price because for every redemption there is a price to pay. Even if you are a kinsman redeemer there is a price to pay. You can ask Boaz in the book of Ruth and he will explain better.

Jesus saw the displeasure in the heart of God caused by those sacrifices of bulls and goats and he responded to it as he said Hebrews 10:5 – ***"wherefore, when he cometh unto the world the world he saith, sacrifices and offering thou wouldest not but a body hast thou prepared me."***

Jesus made the announcement to the world as to prepare their heart for a new change of sacrifice that will replace the former sacrifices. As he realized what was needed, he made a public announcement to the people saying it was needless rushing to bring those sacrifices of bull and goats because the people have turned it into a hypocritical ceremony where people's piety is measured by this outward appearance rather than the inward appearance i.e. their heart.

They have by reason of these sacrifices of bulls and goats turned the house of God which God meant to be a house of prayer to den of thieves, where selling and exchange of money became the order of the day.

So when Jesus visited the temple he discovered men who were still making merchandise of those animals for temple sacrifices. Despite Jesus proclamation they did not give heed to this announcement or teaching by reason of His zeal for God He drove them out of the temple.

Jesus came to do the will of God which will bring pleasure to God and also bring the kind of sacrifices that God required in order to restore man back to glory. Thank God for Jesus because He saw in the volume of the book God has proposed to use Him to accomplish and He responded by making Himself available as the "Lamb of God who takes away the sins of the world".

As in Hebrews 10:8 – 10, - *"Above when he said sacrifice and offering and burnt offerings and offering for sin thou wouldest not neither hadst pleasure therein, which are offered by the law. Then said he, lo I come to do thy will O God, He taketh away the first that he may establish the second. By the which will we are sanctified through the offering of the body of Jesus Christ once for all."*

Have you seen the needs of God and you are keeping quiet about it or you are not doing anything to respond to that need? Remember if you respond actively to the need of God you are bound to receive a reward and exaltation. Without being the lamb of God, Jesus could not have been a name above every other name so that the tongue shall confess that Jesus is Lord.

David had such need and his followers heard this need and responded positively to his need. In 1Chronicles 11:17 – 18, *"And David longed, and said, oh that one would give me drink of water of the well of Bethlehem, that is at the gate! And the three brake through the host of the Philistines, and drew water out of the well of Bethlehem, that was by the gate and took it, and brought it to David: but David would not drink of it, but poured it out to the Lord."*

How do we see the needs of God just like the men that served David and Jesus that saw the need of God. All that know the needs of God either in evangelism, deliverance or righteous living must respond to that need. in Romans 12:1-2 – *"I beseech you therefore brethren, by the mercies of God, that ye present your bodies a living sacrifice, holy, acceptable unto God, which is your reasonable service. And be not conformed to this world but be ye transformed by the renewing of your mind, that ye may prove what is that good, and acceptable and perfect will of God".*

(3) <u>WITHOUT THE SHEDDING OF THE BLOOD THERE IS NO REDEMPTION</u>

In Hebrews 9:27 – *"And almost all things are by the law purged with blood and without shedding of blood is no remission."*

Prior to the fall of man righteousness was part of lifestyle of mankind so the glory not only abound but became a covering over man. but when man sinned, in order to bring back man to God, the law was introduced as to enable man restore his relationship with God.

But the law as we have seen in the scripture above where there is a righteous demand that for sins of man to be appeased there must be a shedding of the blood in order to purge his sins.

Consequently the practice of sacrifices of bulls and goats through burnt offering, peace offering etc came into being. So for a man to have his sins purged he is required to bring any clean animal to the priest who will make the offering on his behalf to God to purge the sins of the sinner.

This became the practice until these sacrifices of bulls and goats were longer pleasant to God and necessitated the coming of Jesus as to become first, a holy animal meant only for God's use, and He was referred to as the Lamb of God and there qualified to shed his blood for the remission of the sins of man.

Hebrews 9:11-14 – *"But Christ being come an high priest of good things to come, by a greater and more perfect tabernacle, not made with hands, that is to say, not of this building, neither by the blood of goats and calves, but by his own blood he entered in once into the holy place, having obtained eternal redemption for us. For if the blood of bulls and of goats and the ashes of a heifer sprinkling the unclean, sanctifieth to the purifying of the flesh; how much more shall the blood of Christ who through the eternal sprit offered himself without spot to God, purge your conscience from dead works to serve the Living God?"*

Since the sacrifices of bulls and goats do not please God, something must as of necessity take its place. The fact that the sacrifices of bulls and goats do not please God does not dispense with the righteous demand of God for the remission of sins.

Without remission of sins there is no redemption, and reconciliation with God. For man to come into grace and obtain mercy from God the shedding of the blood must be done as we can see in Romans 3:25 – *"Whom God hath set forth to be a propitiation through faith in his blood, to declared his righteousness for the remission of sins that are past, through the forbearance of God."*

No man was qualified to be the sacrificial lamb because in iniquity was all men conceived. So God had no other choice than to accept Jesus response to his need. It then became necessary that Jesus must come.

There was no provision for death in heaven as to make Jesus die in heaven for the sake of man. Since death cannot be experienced in heaven there is no other place left for Jesus to use as his sacrificial abode than the earth, so God permitted him to come to the earth so that he can come in the flesh and blood.

If Jesus did not come in flesh and blood the purpose of his coming as to bring the remission of the sins of the world would not have been accomplished.

Jesus was forced to be made lower than the Angels but to come in the form of man that has flesh and blood so that there will be blood to shed and bread of life to eat.

While Jesus was here on earth we saw Him as one of us but with a different mission to salvage those that have the same nature. That is why Jesus coming was not for the salvation of animals, but for man as Jesus came as the Lamb of God. When John the Baptist has this understanding he called Jesus the Lamb of God that taketh away the sins of the world. Many that accepted Him as the Lamb of God received salvation through the forgiveness of sins by the shedding of his blood. In Colossians 1:14 – ***"In whom we have redemption through his blood, even the forgiveness of sins."***

CHAPTER FIVE

HOW DID JESUS PERFORM HIS TASK?

(A) HE CAME IN THE FORM OF MAN

IT IS NOW ESTABLISHED AND ACCEPTED THAT Jesus came in the form of man. He did not look different from the ordinary man neither did he look like UFO (Unidentified Flying Object).

In Philippians 2:6,7,8 we read about Jesus – *"who, being in the form of God, thought it not robbery to be equal with God: but made himself of no reputation and took upon him the form of a servant, and was made in the likeness of men. And being found in fashion as a man he humbled himself and became obedient unto death even the death of the cross."*

Though he originally had the form of God as the scripture described but when it has to do with his coming to the earth he took the form of man that he has come to rescue.

In the Old Testament God made man in His own image but in this new dispensation God took the form or image of man for the salvation of man.

To prove that He had the form of man not just having flesh and blood because there are other animals that have flesh and blood three aspects of man were seen in Him.

Ordinary, a man has body, soul and spirit which other animals do not have. So Jesus manifested his bodily form in these three components of man; spirit, soul and body.

Mathew 26:12 says ***"for in that she hath poured this ointment on my body, she did it for my burial."*** This was the same Mary Magdalene that was looking for the body of Jesus after His resurrection in John 20:13.

Jesus also had a soul when he was living on earth, see John 12:27 – ***"Now is my soul troubled: and what shall I say? Father, save me from this but for this cause came I unto this hour."***

In Luke 23:36 we read ***"And when Jesus had cried with a loud voice he said, father, unto thy hands I commend my spirit and having said thus he gave up the ghost."*** Jesus was complete as a man having body, soul and spirit.

Apart from the above reference he did the things only man can do. So the beginning of Jesus success in fulfilling his God given mandate was his acceptance and actualization of coming in the form of man to redeem man.

If Jesus did not come in the form of man he couldn't have accomplished his mission for the following reasons:

(1) When God created the earth, he gave authority to man represented by Adam to have control and dominion over the earth. So Jesus can only come in the form of man in order to exercise that power and authority given to man. Jesus as a man with the power of God can control nature and elemental beings.

(2) Secondly the man through Adam lost the power and the glory God gave him through subtlety of the devil. Jesus therefore needed to come in the form of a man so that he can qualify to contest the title of the whole earth with the devil. Without being a man he could not have qualified to fight the devil.

(3) It was man that God created and who the devil disgraced. Therefore God needed to use man to disgrace the devil by eventually going to Calvary to purchase for every believer the authority to cast out devil, Mark 16:17 – *"And these signs shall follow them that believe, in my name shall they cast out devils. They shall speak with new tongues."*

(4) Jesus came in the form of man so that the righteous demand of God can be met. God said without the shedding of blood here is no remission of sins. Jesus came in the flesh so that his blood can stand as an atonement for our sins and the blood can become a weapon in our hands to overcome the devil.

(B) HE CAME IN AS A CHILD

Luke 2:7 – *"And she brought forth her firstborn son, and wrapped him in swaddling clothe, and laid him in a manger, because there was no room for them in the inn."*

Also in Luke 2:10-12 – *"And the angel said unto them fear not: for behold, I bring you good tidings of great joy, which shall be to all people. For unto you is born this day in the city of David a Saviour, which is Christ the Lord. And this shall be a sign unto you, ye shall find the babe wrapped in swaddling clothe, lying in a manger."*

Jesus had the option of coming into the word without being a child. He had the power to come and still achieve what he wanted to achieve without being a child.

The bible recorded about a man who had some resemblance of Jesus though there was no established fact that he was Jesus. This man had a record of being in the world just as a king and a priest. This same man had no beginning or end. This same man had no genealogy i.e. he had no father or mother yet he lived here on earth. He was a king here on earth; he was also a priest unto God here on earth.

He had interaction with men on earth; he was seen by men and his office both as a king and a priest and was also recognized even by our patriarch Abraham. This man was called Melchizedek.

Even when Jesus eventually came, the Bible recorded he came as a king and a priest in the order of Melchizedek. See Hebrews 7:1-3 – *"For this Melchizedek, king of Salem, priest of the Most High God, who met Abraham returning from the slaughter of the king and blessed him: to whom also Abraham gave a tenth part of all; first being by interpretation king of righteousness and after that also king of Salem which is king of peace. Without father, without mother, without desent, having neither beginning of days, nor end of life, but made like unto the son of God; abideth a priest continually."*

Also in Hebrews 7:17 – *"for he testifieth, thou art a priest forever after the order of Melchizedek."*

From the above scriptures we have seen that God has the power to allow Jesus to come to the earth like Melchizedek but He chose that Jesus must come in the form of a child. These are reasons one may deduce to support the claim that Melchizedek was a type of Jesus though not stated categorically in the Bible.

We know that Jesus did not send children away from his presence rather that they should allow them come to Him and we are expected by conduct to be like children in acceptance of the word of God, and believe, just like children believe the word of their parents or teachers. In Mathew 18:2-3 – *"And Jesus called a little child unto him and set him in the midst of them and said verily I say unto you, except ye be converted and become as little children, ye shall not enter into the kingdom of heaven."*

Jesus also came as a child to teach us a spiritual principle that every believer must adhere to, it does not matter how old you have been in the Lord. He made us to understand that any person born again, from that moment in the spiritual rating has become a child. And as a spiritual child just like the physical child, you must desire the sincere milk of the word of God to grow just like the physical child will require natural milk or breast milk to survive.

In 1Peter 2:2 we read – *"As newborn babies, desire the sincere milk of the word that ye may grow thereby."* Jesus also studied the word of God quoted it and even reasoned with the elders in the temple concerning the word of God. Let us learn the spiritual significance of Jesus coming like a child and apply it in our lives for maximum appreciation.

(C) **<u>HE SUBJECTED HIMSELF TO EARTHLY PARENTS.</u>** I wouldn't know how Jesus did it. But I believe that is another higher level of humility in display. Jesus who created all things and through him everybody was created including Joseph and Mary nevertheless, submitted himself to the rulership of the earthly parents whom he created.

In Luke 1:30-31 – *"And the angel said unto her fear not, Mary: for thou hast found favour with God. And behold, thou shalt conceive in thy womb, and bring forth a son and shall call his name JESUS.*

Also in Galatians 4:4 – *"But when the fullness of the time was come, God sent forth his son, made of a woman, made under the law."*

Jesus came into the word through earthly parent and he grew under their care and received fame by things he did while he was on earth not by those things he did while in Heaven. Though Jesus was the only begotten son of God – John 3:16 – *"For God so love the word that he gave his only begotten son…"* and he was only accountable to God the father concerning his mission here on earth but he lived with his earthly parents and was subject to them for a period of 30 years before he began his ministry.

When Jesus had occasion to expound the word of God to the people in the temple he was later discovered to be missing out from his parents after the feast in Jerusalem (Which indeed did not go down well with the parents as a result of being left behind in Jerusalem after the feast).When his parents found him, and He went back with them and yet Jesus remained subject to them.

In Luke 2:48 – 51 – *"And when they saw him; they were amazed and his mother said unto him why hast thou this dealt with us? Behold thy father and I have sought thee sorrowing. And he said unto them, how is it that ye sought me? Wist ye not that I must be about my father's business? And they understood not the saying which he spake unto them. And he went down with them and came to Nazareth, and was subject unto them: but his mother kept all these sayings in her heart."*

Jesus was doing His heavenly Father's business but He did not see it as an excuse to be disobedient or not subject to his earthly parents. But when the time came for His ministry, He was no longer under their control because every knowledge or experience He needed, He had learnt while under tutelage.

Anointing does not bring rascality and it is not an excuse for undisciplined life. There is an important role parents either physical or spiritual must play in the life of every serious minded believer. Anointing without character leads to perdition and early destruction of life and ministry. Go and read the account of Samson who though had anointing was not subject to the godly counsel of his parents and he did things contrary to their teaching and ended both his ministry and life catastrophically while his parents were still alive – what a great loss to heaven.

In Proverbs 29:15 – *"the rod and reproof give wisdom but a child left to himself bringeth his mother to shame."*

Your anointing needs both physical and spiritual control. Any man who cannot be subject to the earthly parents cannot be subjected to God.

(D) **HE STARTED HIS MINISTRY**
Jesus from the onset knew he had two major missions here on earth. Apart from going to the cross to die and redeem man, he had a major assignment to raise and train people who will take after Him and continue in the physical where He stopped.

The idea of ministry becomes quite important if the mission of Christ will be spread abroad and received in the heart of men thus achieving the purpose of God.

Without Jesus ministry we would not have known that God loves us and the level of love that God has for us in John 3:16 – *"for God so loved the world…"*

If Jesus had raised disciples without teaching them the word of God and without preparing and equipping them, it would have been a big catastrophe after Jesus had finished his ministry and left.

To really achieve an everlasting effect of His mission He realized the need to start His ministry as part of event to fulfill His divine task.

Jesus ministry and his death on the cross and His resurrection are all important feature of the fulfillment of His task. Jesus attaches so much importance to His ministry to the extent that even after His resurrection He needed to look for His disciples who were scattered during His arrest. He not only restored them to the ministry but also gave them the power to run the ministry.

In Mark 1:14, 15 – *"Now after that John was put in prison Jesus came into Galilee, preaching the gospel of the kingdom of God, and saying the time is fulfilled, and the kingdom of God is at hand: repent ye and believe the gospel.*
Also in Luke 4:14, 15 – *"And Jesus returned in the power of the spirit into Galilee and there went out a fame of him through all the region round about and he taught in their synagogues being glorified of all."*

Jesus set an example we must follow if we are prepared to do the will of God. Jesus including heaven is not expecting any of us to go to the cross and die in order to save ourselves or other mankind because Jesus had paid that costly price for us to benefit from. In Hebrews 9:15 – *"And for this cause he is the mediator of the new testament that by means of death, for the redemption of the transgressions that were under the first testament, they which are called might receive the promise of eternal inheritance."*

Such sacrifice that Jesus did on the cross was once and is not needed for us to do it again in Hebrews 7:27 we read – *"who needeth not daily, as those high priests, to offer up sacrifice first for his own sins, and then for the people's for this he did once, when he offered up himself."*

Running his ministry was a way of bringing the good news to the people which is quite important and highly needed for the people to appreciate His sacrifice on the cross.

The key to receiving and appropriating what Jesus did on the cross lies in carrying out His ministry. That explains why as soon as time was ripe for His ministry to commence, He did it without delay.

Before He left the earth for heaven He expressed the importance and urgency of the ministry to his disciples with great emphasis.

In Mathew 28:18 – 20 – *"And Jesus came and spoke unto them saying, all power is given unto me in heaven and on earth. Go ye therefore and teach all nations baptizing them in the name of the father and of the son and of the Holy Ghost, teaching them to observe all things whatsoever I have commanded you and lo, I am with you always, even unto the end of the world Amen."*

The issue of personal evangelism is serious if we like Jesus, and if we must fulfill our great mission here on earth. Jesus taught the people while He was here and now He is no longer here on earth, he has handed over to us the ministry of reconciliation so we must as a matter of necessity follow it with all diligence. In 2 Corinthians 5:19 – *"To with, that God was in Christ reconciling the world unto Himself, not imputing their trespasses unto them: and hath committed unto us the word of reconciliation.*

We are required as ambassadors of Christ to play our role effectively in order to please God. In 1Corinthians 4:2 – *"Moreover it is required stewards, that a man be found faithful."*

(E)   <u>HE MADE DISCIPLES</u>

In Mathew 4:18 – 20,22 we read – *"And Jesus walking by the sea of Galilee saw two brethren, Simon called Peter, and Andrew his brother, casting a net into the sea, for they were fishers. And he saith unto them, follow me and I will make you fishers of men. And they straightway left their nets, and followed him… And they immediately left the ship and their father, and followed him."*

A ministry without workers already has foundational problem because everything done here on earth is transient, therefore for continuity sake, you must have disciples.

Jesus first began His ministry before he began raising his disciples. You must first have a message before you begin to look for people to receive the message and become messengers of the word.

We are expected to be living epistles unto others, so there is need for certain measure of decorum to be seen in our lives for us to be able to carry them along. Hebrews 12:1 says – *"Wherefore, seeing we also are compassed about with so great a cloud of witnesses, let us lay aside every weight, and the sin which doth so easily beset us, and let run with patience the race that is set before us."*

Jesus knew that we are going to be assessed by our conduct in relation to our faith so he came to raise disciples unto himself. The issue of raising disciples is just beyond preaching to somebody and the person becomes born again.

Because the process of becoming a disciple is not an easy one, it is highly demanding. Definitely your time, money and other resources must be needed. Jesus needs followers who not only learn his lifestyle but will put it into practice. Apart from imitating Jesus lifestyle, discipleship calls for men who will be touched by the message of Jesus and be in a better position to preach the same message to others. In John 1:3 we read – *"That which we have seen and heard declare we unto you, that ye also may have fellowship with us: and truly our fellowship is with the father, and with his son Jesus Christ."*

Jesus also realized the limitation that he had though being God omnipresent still he was indeed limited being a human flesh, so he has a need for people in like fashion to be involved in the dispensation of the good news.

In ministerial work, there is always need for people to be around you, those who can say with all sincerity that what you preach outside is what you are inside. The people of Jesus time though saw him every time preaching in the synagogue yet when the time to arrest him came; they could not differentiate him from his disciples. They needed one of his disciples to identify him. This is a great challenge for servants of God especially in this era that some of us find our bibles too heavy for us to carry hence we need people to deploy who will carry and drop it on the pulpit for us.

In the time of Jesus, he stooped low and washed the feet of his disciples as a symbol of the kind of humility expected from us. But I wonder in this our dispensation how many of us can do the same to our followers. But the Bible said let this mind that is in Christ be found in us.

Jesus needed to raise disciples so that he could impart leadership qualities into their lives and also make them know that only good followers can become good leaders. Moreover if you want to be a leader you must be a servant and must have served others before you expect and receive such corresponding service from others.

There is no success without a successor. Jesus coming and dying for us would not have been a good success if there no disciples. Raising disciples unto himself is part of the accomplishment of his divine agenda here on earth. Are you one of Jesus disciples? Please be one there will be no regrets.

(F)   <u>**HE LEARNT OBEDIENCE THROUGH SUFFERING**</u>

Part of the ministry of Jesus Christ was the ministry of suffering. Paul realized that suffering is an aspect that made Jesus to excel in his ministry and whosoever must excel in his ministry must also be involved in the same ministry of suffering.

Philippians 3:10 says – *"that I am know him, and the power of his resurrection, and the fellowship of his sufferings being made conformable unto his death."* Paul sincerely desired the fellowship of his suffering and indeed he had a full dose of the fellowship of Jesus suffering.

One may begin to imagine how Jesus had to learn obedience through suffering. Lets see Hebrews 5:8 – *"Though he were a son, yet learned he obedience by the things which he suffered."*

Remember Jesus was not forced into coming to the world to save man, he voluntarily accepted to come and save man. He said I have a right to lay down my life and a right to take it up. Looking at it that way, it means Jesus does not have a need in learning obedience because obedience has become a natural consequence of coming on earth.

But the Bible said he learnt obedience through suffering. Remember this obedience is to the heavenly father who also permitted his coming here on earth. Jesus though he is God came and in the flesh and had some fleshly attributes that is prone to disobedience if unchecked, and uncontrolled.

We know that anointing without character destroys the person easily. When God is interested in you there is a wilderness He must take you through. If God can allow Jesus to go to the wilderness by the leading of the Holy Spirit to be tempted by the devil then, you cannot be exempted from this wilderness experience. God wants to achieve something for himself and also in your life and those things must be seen with the eyes of God. In Deuteronomy 8:2-3 we read – ***"And thou shalt remember all the way which the Lord thy God led thee these forty years in the wilderness, to humble thee, and to prove thee, to know what was in thine heart, whether thou wouldest keep his commandment or no: and he humbled thee, and suffered thee to hunger, and fed thee with manna which thou knewest not, neither did thy fathers know; that he might make thee know that man doth not live by bread only but by every word that proceedeth out of the mouth of the Lord doth man live."***

Wilderness as we can see even in scripture quoted above is normally a place of suffering. But the journey through the wilderness is always for a duration of time that can be made longer or shorter by your attitude towards God in relation to your wilderness experience.

Note obedience is a character that requires learning; nobody easily practices obedience without learning it. Some practice it out of fear of harm, while others practice it because of favour or gift they want to receive from you.

But Jesus never practiced obedience for man's fear or favour he wanted from man. he practiced obedience not only because it is his character, but in heaven where he came from, it is a sine qua non for existence and subsistence.

The obedience that Jesus learnt through suffering was just to subject the flesh to the rulership of the spirit through the soul.

Suffering that produces obedience is not suffering that is characterized by a lot of murmuring and grumbling because it cannot satisfy Isaiah 1:19 – *"if ye be willing and obedient, ye shall eat the good of the land."*

The suffering that produces obedience is one that will make you give thanks to God in all situations either in lack or in surplus. Pure obedience is not produced outside suffering rather suffering is the underlining raw material that is used to produce undefiled obedience.

Jesus left us a good example here on earth and we must also learn obedience through suffering which means he accepted suffering as part of his ministry which Paul saw and was eager to partake in the fellowship of that suffering.

Jesus accepting to learn obedience through suffering is part of the test of humility that can be found in a personality like Jesus. How many times have we failed and grumbled in the fellowship of suffering and still want to do greater things that He did? Well God will help us as we learn obedience unto God through suffering.

(G) <u>HE WENTTO THE CROSS</u>

Another important aspect of Jesus ministry or his divine mission is that of going to the cross to die for the sins of the whole world.

He came to carry our sins away and not to go to heaven with the sins rather crucify sin on the cross so that sin shall no longer be a master over man.

Jesus could have died any other type of death but what would have happened to sins and fleshly disposition of man. The requirement of the scripture is that we must crucify fleshly lusts and the only way to crucify sin and fleshly lust is to take it to the cross.

In Mathew 27:32 we see this, - *"And as they came out, they found a man of Cyrene, Simon byname: him the compelled to bear his cross. And when,...* in verse 35 a – *"and they crucified him..."*

Jesus accepted to go to the cross because of the importance and mystery behind his going to the cross. He could have insisted that he will die without going to the cross. He could have incited a fight in Gethsemane which would have resulted to his death since he knew and had accepted to die but despite all these options, he elected and accepted to go to the cross.

In Hebrew 12:2 we read – *"Looking unto Jesus the author and finisher of our faith; who for the joy that was set before him endured the cross, despising the shame, and is set down at the right hand of the throne of God."*

There was a joy that was set for Jesus and there is a joy that is set for that man who carries his accepted and divine given cross and follows Jesus.

Jesus went to the cross not primarily for the purpose of the joy that was set before him because he had always had joy and glory with God the father before he came to the earth.

He even said in John 17 that God should restore the glory he had with him before he came on his missionary journey here on earth. But the purpose of going to the cross was part of the fulfillment of his divine mandate and for the benefit of mankind.

While Jesus was in Gethsemane he saw the cross, he saw the sufferings, he saw the shame, even as flesh, he asked God if he could still perform his work without drinking the cup of the cross. But he knew there was no other way out so he accepted to go to the cross.

Jesus weighs the benefits of the cross to man against the suffering associated with the cross. He finally decided to go to the cross because of the benefits of the cross to mankind.

The work Jesus came to do here on earth was like a missionary journey, which started as he came in the form of man. From there he did a lot of things, which culminated in his going to the cross.

Even at the cross he had opportunity to save one of the worst criminals who also was crucified along side with him. He gave us a sample of what he had come to the world to do and the benefit of the cross.

If Jesus while still on the cross and a promise of eternal life is made and guaranteed for a man, a criminal for that matter, then what he is doing now that he is in heaven, the pages of this book will not be enough to write them down.

Thanks' be to God that Jesus came and went to the cross.

CHAPTER SIX

THE MYSTERY OF THE CROSS AND CALVARY

(A) THE JOURNEY TO THE CROSS BEGAN AT GETHSEMANE

There is a mystery behind the cross and Calvary. Jesus would have chosen any other type of death either by hanging or by stoning to death – this was rather recommended by the Law of Moses. There is a purpose for the Jews to choose the manner of punishment peculiar to the Roman Empire rather than the one prevailing among the Jews.

It could be said that the allegation against Jesus was that he offended the Law of Moses, which is against Jewish laws, an offence which was not against the Roman laws of any Roman citizen but against the Jews.

Even the Sanhedrin could not allow the punishment governing the Jewish law to prevail despite their knowledge of the law. It is like where a man committed a crime against French laws and was judged by Nigerian laws and punishment meted accordingly.

With God, there is a purpose for everything, why was there this so called *"abnormality"*; God permitted it for some reasons we are going to enumerate later in this chapter.

Before, Jesus went to the cross; there was a spiritual preparation for that journey he was to embark on.

Jesus went to a Garden though not Garden of Eden and he wasn't in this Garden to look for apples or fruits to eat and play around. He wasn't in this Garden for love affair; he also wasn't in this Garden to preach, heal or raise the dead or perhaps feed the thousand people that milked around him.

Even in the visit to the Garden, the crowd was not there except very close partners in the ministry he was trying to bring in as his prayer partners and teach the need to have prayer partners and the importance of corporate prayers done in the secret, in the quietness of environment. The Bible said Jesus took some disciples and visited this Garden and this Garden is called The Garden of Gethsemane.

We read in Mathew 26:36-40 – *"Then cometh Jesus with them unto a place called Gethsemane, and saith unto the disciples, sit ye here, while I go and pray yonder. And he took with him Peter and the two sons of Zebedee and began to be sorrowful and very heavy. Then saith he unto them, my soul is exceeding sorrowful, even unto death: tarry ye here and watch with me. And he went a little further, and fell on his face, and prayed, saying o my father, if it be possible, let this cup pass from me: nevertheless, not as I will but as thou wilt. And he cometh unto the disciples, and findeth them asleep and saith unto Peter, what could ye not watch with me one hour?"*

You discovered that in the issue of going to Gethsemane it was Jesus that took his disciples into the Garden unlike when Jesus went to the wilderness to be tempted by the devil, he was led into it by the Holy Spirit. It then means on the issue of wilderness experience it is most often the Holy Spirit that takes us into the wilderness to try and build up our faith.

While on the issue of prayers for preparation for the fulfillment of one's vision or mission you are the one that will make conscientious effort to go into the prayer either you do it alone or you go with some people (i.e. corporate prayers).

Thought Jesus entered into the Garden with his disciples who were the inner caucus members of his ministry, they were not of any assistance to him to the realization of his mission in the Garden. But there is a big lesson to learn from this experience. Jesus though did not receive support or co-operation from his ministry partners yet he refused to be deterred by their poor performance and still went ahead to fulfill his mission in the garden.

Jesus became sorrowful and very heavy in the place of prayer that is to tell us that sometimes the Holy Spirit can lay it in our heart about some sorrowful events in the course of the fulfillment of our mission, sometimes the burden may be so heavy that the Holy Spirit may lead you into praying seriously about the heaviness and sorrowfulness of the problem.

Remember that prayers are meant to work in two dimensions: to remove heavy burden and sorrows or to make it light when you encounter them.

We later saw during Jesus journey to the cross as he was given heavy cross to carry that he fell under the cross several times and a human assistance was given to him. Moreover, he was subjected to sorrowful and horrible experiences that people and passer-by including the women started weeping for him.

But because he has already been spiritually fortified in the Garden as to prepare him for this event, he could no longer feel the impact of sorrow like the women hence he told them that they should not weep for him but weep for themselves.

The place of Gethsemane is also a place of negotiation and understanding of vision and mission. When Jesus went to the Garden he was shown the event that will soon befall him in the accomplishment of his mission here on earth.

He called God into a negotiating table and asked God if it was possible, he could still achieve his mission without tasting the bitter experience lined up for him but when he understood God's perfect intention and what He wanted to achieve by his experiencing death in that form, he submitted to the perfect will of God. A place of prayer is for you to understand God's will for you and sometimes some of the things that may befall you before the promises of God will come to manifestation in your life.

The place of prayer helps you to prepare and be strong against any event that may appear unpleasant to you so that the peace that will reign in your life when those things are happening around you will be the peace that passeth all understanding both to you and those around you.

It is important to know that Jesus going to Gethsemane left us an example to follow. Remember that after the prayers Jesus made in the Garden of Gethsemane, there was no record of proper prayer made again by him from the time he left Gethsemane till when he was hanged on the cross. The only short prayer he muttered while on the cross was *"father unto your hand I commit my soul."*

We need to realize from this Jesus experience that we don't have to wait until problems come before we start praying. This is because most often when we are with the problems we don't have the stamina and concentration to pray rather we will be running around seeking for solution to our problem.

But if we can pray ahead of problems, the Holy Spirit will either reveal it to us as to prayerfully take care of the problems or prepare us to face the problems squarely with ease and peace of mind because your flesh may not permit you to muster enough strength and courage to pray.

In the Garden of Gethsemane Jesus laid a foundation both for personal prayers and corporate prayers. Both of which are sine qua non for the fulfillment of your mission. They are all important in the actualization of your God given vision.

Jesus went ahead to pray, he refused to be distracted by his follower's sleep. He refused to be distracted by their weakness because he knew that would mar his mission.

You now discover that it was only Jesus that prayed in Gethsemane while the disciples that went with him slept away their time because they did not understand why they should be in Gethsemane. As for the disciples of Jesus, they were only used to receiving healing, miracles or material things. They were not interested in paying the price to be channels of these blessings they long for. That is why when Jesus left them in the Garden to go beyond to pray, they never bothered or sought to follow him as to pray along with him.

But we know there have been instances that Jesus left them in the past to go to another region to preach. They were still able to discover the place and follow because they were looking for bread and butter miracles but when it had to do with prayers, they were okay where Jesus left them. This goes to explain why nothing was heard about them after the incident at Gethsemane.

Today all over the world, we still have the same group of believers (though in majority) who do not want to come to the place of prayer, who do not want to pay the price but only move from one place to the other or from one ministry to the other looking for miracles without realizing that God had made them instruments of blessing but are not ready or patient enough to be used by God to affect other lives positively.

Even the members of the inner circle of Jesus ministry who went to sleep when they were supposed to be praying could not get the spiritual stamina to resist temptation when it came. That was why Peter who could not then depend upon his spiritual vigour but had no other choice than to depend on his sword – instrument of violence.

Jesus did not waste time to teach Peter a great lesson that henceforth the weapons of our warfare are not carnal but mighty through God to the pulling down of strong holds. Peter and others could not do any other spiritual work after the Gethsemane experience because when they were supposed to be praying, they were sleeping. That is why they decided to go back to their fishing business but Jesus came to re-instate them and show them the way forward in their ministry.

Some today are already out of being fishers of men and have fallen back to fishers of fish to make money. Some have lost hope in the vision God gave them, some are already confused because they do not know the way forward. Don't bother, what you need to do is to go back to your own Gethsemane that is a place of prayer to seek God with all your heart, you will definitely find him. He said in Deut. 4:29 *"But if from thence thou shall seek the Lord thy God, thou shalt find him, if thou shalt seek him with all thy heart and with all thy soul.*

Moreover if you bring in God in whatever you are doing, he will surely help you and direct you on what to do. See Proverbs 3:6 – *"In all thy ways acknowledge him, and he shall direct thy ways."*

But Jesus who refused to be distracted in the place of prayer with help of the Holy Spirit was able to accomplish his mission. He said *"I have overcome the world."* Do you want to overcome the world and fulfill your mission? You need to remember the experience at Gethsemane and practice it continuously.

(B) <u>THE PUBLIC HYPOCRITICAL TRIAL OF JESUS</u>

When Jesus was arrested by the Jews at Gethsemane after his prayer, he was led to Pontus Pilate for trial.

We read in John 18:28-32 – *"Then led they Jesus from Caiaphas unto the hall of judgment: and it was early and they themselves went not into the judgment hall lest they should be defiled but that they might eat the Passover. Pilate then went out unto them and said unto him, if he were not a male factor, we would not have delivered him up unto thee. Then said Pilate unto them, take ye him and judge him according to your law. The Jews therefore said unto him. It is not lawful for us to put any man to death: that the saying of Jesus might be fulfilled which he spake signifying what death he should die."*

The above verse depicts the hypocritical trial that followed Jesus while he was here on earth by the same people he came to save. The trial is replete with so many abuses of court or trial process involved in the trial of a person accused of criminal offence.

In a criminal matter against an individual, one person should stand as the complainant, while others may be his witnesses. Even if it involves an offence against the entire nation like the one against Jesus, the state or the nation will be represented by person employed by the state with professional bias in the area of judicial trials and processes.

But the trial of Jesus witnessed a mob prosecution and a mob presentation of charges. It is also hypocritical and against criminal procedure in the sense that the accusers or complainant in the case against Jesus refused to come into the Court Hall for the prosecution of the case.

Ironically, the judge had to go outside the Court room to hear the charge against Jesus and come into the Court room to continue the trial of the accused.

The accused was never given opportunity to cross-examine the complainant and his witnesses as to test the veracity of their evidence.

The Jew also discovered that what they were doing were not lawful and they refused that Jesus should be judged according to their own law. Because if that was done, definitely Jesus would have been set free. So Jesus committed offence against a particular nation with their own law but was prosecuted on account of another law governing a different set of people.

The questions that were thrown at Jesus was never done by the prosecutor or prosecuting counsel but it was the same judge after hearing the charge against Jesus that came to prosecute the charge and eventually gave judgment. This is the kind of court our journalist describes as a Kangaroo Court.

Unfortunately Pilate discovered that the evidence before him was not weighty enough to convict Jesus of the said offence see John 18:38 – *"Pilate saith unto him what is truth? And when he had said this he went out again unto the Jews, and saith unto them I find in him no fault at all."*

The question now is what will make a judge who did not find the accused to have committed the offence leveled against him go ahead and release an already convicted person who indeed committed grievous offence? As we have recorded in Luke 23:25 – *"And he released unto them him that for sedition and murder was cast into prison, whom they had desired; but he delivered Jesus to their will."*

And Jesus took the place of Barabbas and was sentenced to death.

Jesus was not given the opportunity of being taken to prison since he was taking the position of Barabbas but straightway he was condemned and the condemnation was to be carried out immediately.

Why did Jesus allow himself to be subject to this kind of public hypocritical trial? One can draw some strong reasons from the events that took place. The first being that Jesus had announced the kind of death he would experience, so event must conform to the word of the master. John 18:32 – *"That the saying of Jesus might be fulfilled, which he spake, signifying what death he should die."*

The second reason being that Jesus must be tried according to the Roman law so that his sentence will also be executed according Roman Laws or custom. In Jewish

Law there is no provision for death through crucifixion. Without going through crucifixion, the purpose of Jesus death may not be fully realized. Because death on the cross is God's divine plan for the total package for the salvation of man.

The third lesson is that Jesus took Barabbas fall and death sentence Isaiah 53:4-5 – *"surely he hath borne our griefs and carried our sorrows: yet we did esteem him stricken, smitten of God, and afflicted. But he was wounded for our transgression, he was bruised for our iniquities; the chastisement of our peace was upon him: and with his stripes we are healed."*

The event that made the Jews demand the release of a condemned murderer in place of Jesus was indeed a prophetic one signifying what Jesus came to do for the entire world. For by our Adamic nature we are all condemned and fallen short of the glory of God. We are appointed to die and go to hell, but Jesus came to take our place our griefs and sorrows. Jesus took my place that I may both live here on earth and have a place in heaven thereafter.

The fourth lesson to be derived from the trial is the false accusation leveled against Jesus. It is to remind us that as followers of Jesus we are expected to receive such false accusation from the devil. Revelations 12:10 states *"And I heard a loud voice saying in heaven, now is come salvation, and strength and the kingdom of our God, and the power of Christ: for the accuser of our brethren is cast down, which accused them before our God day and night."* It should not be in our place to murmur or complain when the devil or his human agent brings false accusation against us. In such situation once we have stated the position of things, we are then to keep quiet and allow God to vindicate us.

The fifth lesson from Jesus experience of this hypocritical trial is that Jesus stuck to the truth whereby, Pilate discovered that he did not commit any offence that deserved death. John 18:37 puts it this way, ***"Pilate therefore said unto him, art thou a king then? Jesus answered; thou sayest that I am a king. To this end was I born, and for this cause came I into the world, that I should bear witness unto the truth. Everyone that is of the truth heareth my voice."***

We should not and also don't expect the word to understand us or follow our argument because they are not of the truth. It is only those that belong to the truth that will understand our position and hear our voice.

Sixthly, we need to understand that Jesus was taken to a court where the Jew used sentiments and not evidence of the law to obtain judgment. Sometimes the accuser of the brethren, the human agent may take our names or properties to occultic group for screening in order to inflict on us injury or pass judgment of barrenness or death upon us.

Here also we are not expected to worry or get frightened what is expected of us as Christians is to maintain the truth and walk in righteousness for God had made provision for our victory Isaiah 54:17 tells us – ***"No weapon that is formed against thee shall prosper, and every tongue that shall rise up against thee in judgment thou shall condemn. This is the heritage of the servant of the Lord and their righteousness is of me, saith the Lord."***

Finally the Jews were making a demand for the life of Jesus which they knew was illegal, yet they pressed on. John 18:31 put it this way, – *"Then said Pilate unto them, take ye him and judge him according to your law. The Jews therefore said unto him, it is not lawful for us to put any man to death."*

It is like asking the Judge to impose a punishment that is not provided by the law or outside the ambit of the law upon which the offender is tried. Despite the fact that the punishment demanded by the Jews was not provided for in their law, it was granted unto them.

It is also for us to know that sometimes the devil or his human agent may demand punishment for us that is against the word of God, this should not bother us. Even though Pilate sat as a judge over Jesus, he cannot sit as a judge over our own case. The same Jesus is now our advocate though none was provided for him in his time, God is sitting as a Judge over our matters and is now asking a question in Romans 8.33-34 – *"who shall lay anything to the charge of God's elect? It is God that justifieth, who is he that condemneth? It is Christ that died, yea rather, that is risen again who is even at the right hand of God who also maketh intercession for us."*

We need to relax and depend upon the word of God as our rock of salvation. God further gave us a full assurance in Lamentation 3:37 – *"who is he that saith and it cometh to pass, when the Lord commandeth it not."*
Romans 8:1 – *"There is therefore now no condemnation to them which are in Christ Jesus who walk not after the flesh, but after the spirit."*

(C) <u>THE JOURNEY TO THE CROSS</u>

There is no ceremony associated with a condemned man on his journey to his final resting place. But in the case of Jesus we saw multitude of people that were involved in the hypocritical trial of Jesus who also followed in the ceremony for his crucifixion.

Luke 23:27 – *"And there followed him a great company of people, and of women, which also bewailed and lamented him."* The people were happy, that finally Jesus had been nabbed soon they will get rid of him. The rulers were happy that a man who is fast taking their position in spiritual matters will soon be laid to rest. One of them even made a prophetic statement that was indeed beneficial to the entire race. In John 18:14 we read – *"Now Caiphas was he, which gave counsel to the Jews, that it was expedient that one man should die for the people."*

On the part of Pontus Pilate it was also a good riddance for Jesus to die in order to avert any form of insurrection against the constituted authorities by the Jews. Despite the warning by the wife of Pilate in Mathew 27:19 – *he still went ahead to hand Jesus over to his accusers.*

Most often when a criminal is condemned, he will be sent to the prison before execution is ordered by the executive arm of Government. But in the case of Jesus it was a direct movement from the place of judgment to the place of execution.

It is indeed to stop any appeal that may arise from the judgment of Pontus Pilate, which is replete with judicial error. It is a judgment that is against equity, good conscience and natural justice. Even the common law or canon law will not give room for such judgment.

Nevertheless, it has been given and on the same date the same complainant in the case against Jesus were the same executors of Jesus. The haste in which this journey commenced has a lot of implications. It is worthy to note that Jesus allowed this journey, if not, He has the power to do one thing or the other to defend himself as He said in John 18:36 – *"Jesus answered, my kingdom is not of this world: if my kingdom were of this world, then would my servant fight, that I should not be delivered to the Jews: but now is my kingdom not from thence."*

Jesus knew the importance of the journey to the cross. He also knew the events that would herald the journey to the cross and the resultant effects of this journey.

He knew that without this journey the event would not have taken place and the eternal agenda of God would have been adversely affected or not completed.

Note that for any journey the Holy Spirit subjects you to as a believer either in carrying your cross, or entering into your promised land, there is something God wants to achieve by that.

The journey to the cross was very short though excruciating to Jesus. It was short because Jesus humbly submitted to the journey without undue pressure or resistance. Philippians 2:5-11 – *"let this mind be in you, which was also in Christ Jesus who, being in the form of God thought it not robbery to be equal with God: but made himself of no reputation, and took upon him the form of a servant, and was made in the likeness of men being found in fashion as a man, <u>he humbled himself, and became obedient unto death</u>, even the death of the cross. Wherefore, God also hath highly exalted him, and given him a name which is above every name…"*

For us as believers there is a journey we must undertake like Jesus. It may be a journey with our cross or a journey through the wilderness to the promise land.

If Jesus did not escape the journey, you too cannot escape it. So get yourself prepared for the journey or if you are already in it, then you need to allow the same mind that was in Jesus to be in you. That is the only way to achieving the desired result and getting it accomplished quicker.

Note also that Jesus did not go on the journey alone. He was accompanied by two sets of people. Firstly, he was accompanied by his executioners and secondly by his mockers and despisers.

In your journey be rest assured that you will also be accompanied by devil whose responsibility is to tell you among other things how God has abandoned you and allowed you to suffer when you are not supposed to suffer. He will tell you the need to doubt the word of God by reminding you how long the word of God has stayed to be unfulfilled in your life. He can even quote the scriptures to you that *"can the dead praise God?"* is it when you have died that your miracle will come? He will remind you of your age if your desire is in the area of marriage or fruitfulness. He will bring a lot of ministrations to discourage you and turn your back to God.

The other set of people are your mockers and despisers whose job is to mock you. The only thing they will say is that there is no other thing you do rather than carry your bible and sleep in the church. They will ask you if you think that God still drops manna from heaven. They will also quote the scripture for you *"that if you do not work you should not eat."* They will call you lazy man and all sorts names.

These two sets of people are all needed in this journey so that the word of God will come to pass. There is a testimony that God has kept for you at the end of the journey and that is the testimony you will use to overcome the devil see Revelations 12:11 – *"And they overcame him by the blood of the lamb and <u>by the word of their testimony</u>; and they loved not their lives unto the death."*

The second set of mockers and despisers are also needed because at the end, they will see the table of blessing that God had prepared for you even in the midst of your adversaries. Ps. 23:5 – *"Thou prepares a table before me in the presence of mine enemies: thou anointest my head with oil; my cup runneth over."*

The journey is divine; allow it in your life just as Jesus without compulsion allowed it. Even when you have an option don't follow it as long as God had permitted the journey. It is a journey of obedience and humility just as Jesus obeyed and God elevated Him. Philippians 2:9 – *"Wherefore God also hath highly exalted him and given him a name which is above every name."*

God is ready to exalt you. Allow the journey to be short though it sometimes may be shameful, sorrowful and excruciating but there is a glory reserved for you after the successful journey.

(D) <u>THE EVENT OF THE JOURNEY TO THE CROSS</u>

For everything in God's agenda there is a purpose. As long as God is concerned, He has destined all events to work out for good for us. See Rom. 8:28 – *"And we know*

*that all things work together for good to them that love
God to them who are the called according to His purpose.*

When Paul was writing to the Romans, he was indeed bringing deep spiritual truth to them. He stated that we know all things work together for good. Paul was emphasizing the point that it is not only himself that knows but that *"we"* in that verse is an indication that Paul was not the only person that had this knowledge. It has become a common knowledge among some of them that have tested or have experienced God.

The knowing in this verse is beyond head knowledge or by reading it in a Christian or testimony magazine. It is a knowledge that was read in the book and manifested in the physical in the life of that person that read it.

The *"all things"* here refers to all the events that are happening around you now or had happened in your life. Whether you pray for it or not the power of God will draw them together and they will start working together. No matter how bad or evil those events may all look, the end result of their working together is to produce good for you.

Remember that the *"good"* that all these events produce is not of general application to everybody. It is only meant for those *"that love God"* and who are *"called according to his purpose"*. What this means cannot be explained in this book so that there wouldn't be much digression from the topic.

So in the event of the journey to the cross there is no singular event among them that are palatable, encouraging or consoling. All tend to graduate from bad to worse but at the end of it all, they were not only good for Jesus but also good for all his followers and as many that received Him or believe in Him.

In Mathew 27:26 we read – *"Then released he Barabbas unto them and when he had scourged Jesus, he delivered him to be crucified. Then the soldiers of the governor took Jesus into the common Hall and gather unto him the whole band of soldiers. And they stripped him and put on him a scarlet robe. And when they had platted a crown of thorns, they put upon his head and a reed in his right hand and they bowed the knee before him and mocked him saying, Hail, king of the Jews! And they spit upon him, and took the reed, and smote him on the head. And after that they had mocked Him, they took the robe off from him, and put own raiment on him and let him away to crucify him. And as they came out, they found a man of Cyrene, Simon by name: him, they compelled to bear his cross."*

These events were also recorded in the other synoptic gospel. It may not be necessary to write down all of them in this book. However we may have to make references to them for further reading.

All the event regarding the journey to the cross were actually carried out by human agents and none posed any surprise to God or Jesus, as some of the prophets of the old testament prophesied about such event before they took place.

One of the events that took place in this journey was that Jesus was flogged i.e. scourged as in Mathew 27:26. However the prophets saw the event before it took place in Isaiah 50:6 – *"I gave my back to the smiters…* Also in Isa. 53:4-5 – *"surely he hath borne our griefs and carried our sorrows: yet we did esteem him striken, smitten of God, and afflicted. But he was wounded for our transgressions, he was bruised for our iniquities, the chastisement of our peace was upon him and with his stripes we are healed."* Jesus allowed them to flog him because it has divine approval.

Secondly, He was stripped of his clothing as recorded in Mathew 27:28 – *"And they stripped him…"* Not only did they strip him, they also parted and shared his garment by casting lots. In Ps. 22:18 – *"they part my garments among them and cast lots upon my vesture."*

Thirdly, they plated a crown of thorns and put it on Jesus head as in Mathew 27:29 – *"And when they had platted a crown of thorns they put it upon his head."*

In Isa. 53:5 – *"But he was wounded for our transgression, he was bruised for our iniquities…"*

The fourth event was they mocked Jesus in Mathew 27:29 – *"…and they bowed the knee before him, and mocked him, saying Hail, king of the Jews."* However in Ps. 22:6-8 – *"But I am a worm, and no man, a reproach of men, and despised of the people. All they that see me laugh me to scorn: they shoot out the lip, they shake the head, saying: He trusted on the Lord that he would deliver him: let him deliver him, seeing he delighted in him."*

The fifth event was that they spat upon him and smote upon his head. In Mathew 27:30 – *"And they spit upon him, and took the reed, and smote him on the head."* This was also prophesized by prophet Isaiah in Isaiah 50:6 – *"I gave my back to the smiters, and my cheeks to them that plucked off the hair: I hid not my face from shame and spitting."*

The sixth event on this same journey was that He was blind folded as in Luke 22:64 – *"And when they had blindfolded him, they struck him on the face, and asked him, saying prophesy, who is it that smote thee?"*

The seventh event was as recorded in Luke 22:65 – *"And many other things blasphemously spake they against him."* They went on saying things that were not good enough to put down on the print rather the writers generalized things they said.

Finally Simon was conscripted to carry Jesus cross as a way of assisting him see Mathew 27:32 – *"And as they came out, they found a man of Cyrene, Simon by name: him they compelled to bear his cross."*

(E) <u>THE RESULTS OF THE EVENTS TO THE CROSS.</u>

God, we know is a God of purpose. Whatever thing God does, He has the welfare of His children at heart.

Jesus had the privilege of knowing the purpose of God for His children. Even when the Bible said that God so loved the world that He gave his son. Jesus knew that every event is geared towards the realization of that statement.

When Jesus was in Gethsemane negotiating His divine mission, He perceived the events that were awaiting Him beginning from Gethsemane to his journey on the cross. He remembered the benefits mankind will derive from those events and the desires of God pertaining to those events, He submitted to the will of God.

The events were not ordinary. They were permitted to bring desired results. Such results we shall quickly look at in Rom. 5:12 – *"wherefore, as by one man sin entered into the world, and death by sin; and so death passed upon all men, for that all have sinned."*

Through Adam's sin so many things were introduced into the world and into the life of mankind. The events of the journey to the cross took care of those things introduced by Adam's fall and consequences of those fall. For example nakedness was introduced in Gen. 3:7 – *"And the eyes of them both were opened, and they knew that they were naked, and they sewed fig leaves together, and made themselves aprons."*

The result of one of the events was to deal with the issue of nakedness in the life of man. Jesus suffered nakedness so as to provide a succor for every nakedness believer would pass through in the journey to the Promised Land. In John 19:23 we read – *"Then the soldiers, when they had crucified Jesus, took his garments, and made four parts, to every soldier a part and also his coat."*

Another thing the fall of man introduced was sorrow and curses in Gen. 3:17 – *"And unto Adam he said, because thou has hearkened unto the voice of thy wife, and hast eaten of the tree, of saying, thou shalt not eat of it: cursed is the ground for thy sake; in sorrow shalt thou eat of it all the days of thy life."*

Jesus indeed experienced sorrows and suffered severally for the sake of mankind so as to deliver us from various sorrows the devil had lined up for us, hence he paid the price in Isa. 53:3 – *"He is despised and rejected of men; a man of sorrows, and acquainted with grief: and we hid as it were our faces from him; he was despised, and we esteemed him not."*

The resultant effect of the sins of Adam was the introduction of thorns in the affairs of man in order to hinder growth and financial blessings Gen. 3:18 – ***"Thorns also and thistles shall it bring forth to thee and thou shalt eat the herb of the field."*** – With this, every effort of man does not yield the desired results. Blessing do not manifest to the fullest. It became half measure of blessing. But Jesus used this event to collect all the thorns and thistles that have stood in the way of man to financial breakthrough and put it on his head as a crown. John 19:5 – ***"Then came Jesus forth, wearing the crown of thorns and the purple robe. And Pilate unto Him behold the man."***

Jesus knowing that He was going to the cross to deal with everything that had hitherto stood in the way of man, being reconciled back to God also allowed the thorns of judgment to come along so that he would sacrifice it on the cross.

Today, the thorns of the devil, the thorns of curses have no place in our business or marriages we have been delivered from financial bondage and stagnation occasioned by the thorns on the ground. As we appropriate unto ourselves what Jesus did on the cross the thorns have no power over our finances or blessings. Moreover, the head that once was crowned with thorns is crowned with glory now.

In Luke 23:36 – ***"And the soldiers mocked him, coming to him, and offering him vinegar."***

It was not only the soldiers that mocked Jesus, the watching crowd mocked him, Luck 23:35; the chief priest mocked him – Mt. 27:44.

Jesus received all these mockery as to leave an example for us to follow. In time to come this same set of people that mocked Jesus will also exalt him and call him Lord.

So as a believer you should expect mockery from different quarters. The soldiers represent the Government. You may come in direct conflict with the Government when you denounce their practices. The crowd watching your Christian life will also mock you especially when things are not moving well for you. Remember the Bible said we are surrounded with great cloud of witnesses. The chief priest in this context represents fellow believers and ministers who also may mock you when they don't understand your vision or mission or even when things are not working out for you. They may even call you a lazy person. The thief represents the heathen or unbelievers; definitely it is their ministry to mock the children of God. Even in Abraham's household, Ishmael and his mother despised and mocked the son of promise Isaac. Because you are a child of promise, a child of covenant, the unbelievers are bound to mock you but don't worry the Bible said in Isa. 126:1-3 – *"when the Lord turned again the captivity of Zion, we were like them that dream. Then was our mouth filled with laughter, and our tongue with singing: <u>Then said they among the heathen</u>, the Lord hath done great things for them. The Lord hath done great things for us, whereof we glad.*

Jesus was also spat upon and He carried his own spit and your own to the cross and cleansed them with his blood so that you are cleansed from spiritual and physical spit any man or woman may spit upon you.

In Mathew 27:26 – *"Then released he Barabbas unto them; and when he had scorged Jesus, he delivered him to be crucified."*

Jesus was flogged. He was beaten and there were stripes from the flogging on his body. The stripes made provision for our healing from all types of sickness or diseases be it Aids, leprosy etc. in 1Pet. 2:24 – *"Who his own self bare our sins in his own body on the tree, that we, being dead to sins should live unto righteousness: <u>By whose stripes</u> ye were healed."* Also read Isaiah 53:5 – *"But he wounded for our transgressions he was bruised for our iniquities, the chastisement of our peace was upon him and with his stripes we are healed."*

It is now obvious that all that Jesus suffered on his way to Calvary is for our benefits. The result is to give us a total package of salvation.

It is not only a salvation that saves us from our sins. But a salvation that attracts blessings, prosperity and healing unto as many that have genuinely received the salvation of God through Jesus Christ.

(F) <u>THE RESULT OF CALVARY</u>

Isa. 53:4-7 says *"surely he hath borne our griefs, and carried our sorrows: yet we did esteem him striken, smitten of God, and afflicted. But he was wounded for our transgression, he was bruised for our iniquities; the chastisement of our peace was upon him: and with his stripes we are healed. All we like sheep have gone astray; we have turned everyone to his own way; and the Lord hath laid on him the iniquity of us all. He was oppressed, and he was afflicted, yet He opened not his mouth: He is brought as a lamb to the slaughter, and as a sheep before her shearers is dumb, so He openeth not His mouth."*

Also in Ps. 22:6-8 – *"But I am a worm and no man; a reproach of men, and despised of the people. All they that see me laugh me to scorn: they shoot out the lip, they shake the head, saying, he trusted on the Lord that he would deliver him: let him deliver him, seeing he delighted in him."*

The death of Jesus was not a surprise to Jesus, it was not also a surprise to the prophets of the Old Testament they prophesied exactly what Jesus encountered. Today it is a well-known fact that Jesus actually went to the cross to die. When you look at the cross-section of religious group, you will see them decorating their alters or church building with a cross or a cross that has the image of man (supposedly referred to as Jesus) on that cross.

It is now an accepted fact that Jesus on his own accord went to Calvary to die on the cross for the benefit of all.

Before the death on the cross Jesus informed His disciples about his death and resurrection. In Matt. 17:22, 23 – *"And while they abode in Galilee, Jesus said unto them the son of man shall be betrayed into the hands of men: and they shall kill him, and third day he shall be raised again. And they were exceeding sorry."*

The fulfillment of the above mentioned scripture came to pass in the life of Jesus Christ as we can see in John 19:16-18 – *"Then delivered he him therefore unto them to be crucified. And they took Jesus and led him away. And he bearing his went forth into a place called the place of skull, which called in the Hebrew Golgotha: Where they crucified him, and two other with him, on either side one, and Jesus in the midst.*

Further in verse 32-33 of John 19 stated – *"then came the soldiers, and brake the legs of the first, and of the other which was crucified with him. But when they came to Jesus, and saw that he was dead already, they brake not his legs."*

The death of Jesus was also recorded in Luke 23:33 – *"And when they were come to the place which is called Calvary, there they crucified him, and the malefactors, one on the right hand and the other on the left."*

Jesus going to the cross to die is for everybody. Salvation will definitely follow as many that shall appropriate unto their life what Jesus did on the Calvary for his death is for the benefit of all, see Heb. 2:9 – *"But we see Jesus, who was made a little lower than the angels for the suffering of death crowned with glory and honour; that he by the grace of God should taste death for every man."*

Like we said earlier, Jesus would have chosen any type of death different from going to the cross. But He decided to allow the death he had accepted to be confirmed by heavenly requirement. In Hebrews 8:5 – *"Who serve unto the example and shadow of heavenly things as Moses was admonished of God when he was about to make the tabernacle. For see saith he, that thou make all things according to the pattern shewed to thee in the mount."* This scripture referred to Moses but Jesus also followed the spiritual principles outlined in that scriptures.

When Jesus was in Gethsemane praying, He desired to have the cup pass without his drinking it, but when He saw the heavenly pattern of his death and the resultant effect upon mankind, He decided to accept his death to be according to the pattern shown unto Him in his mount of prayer – Gethsemane.

God does not do anything without a purpose. For John 3:16 said – *"for God so love the world that He gave his only begotten son…"* so that the people will not perish.

Everything God did was to actualize these desires of God so that man will not perish but have eternal life.

Jesus death on the cross was not ordinary. His death brought a lot of results to mankind, which we may enumerate; some among which are as follows:

Jesus hath borne our grief. Every grief that the devil has subjected any child of God to, Jesus said those griefs are to be on him. So that when situations around us tend to show that we are passing through some grief moment either in our marriage or business or spiritual life, we may not experience the grief the way the enemy meant it.

Sometimes we see ourselves smiling in time of grief, sometimes we see ourselves praising God with a genuine heart. All is because Jesus had borne our grief. In a moment of grief you see us professing hope knowing fully well that all is not lost that God has ability to repair or replenish that which is lost. Jesus is announcing to us from the cross, grieve no more there is hope, for we are more than a conqueror and no weapon fashioned against us shall prosper. Though they speak the word (negative verdict) it shall not come to pass because God is with us. Alleluia!

One other benefit of Calvary is that Jesus took upon himself sorrows. In the life of every believer there are events that the devil had lined up in bringing sorrows to them. He can attack your business, marriage, children or extended family all in a bid to afflict you with sorrows.

My Brother and my sister, I have good news for you. I am happy to announce to you that Jesus while on Calvary carried our sorrows. The word "*sorrows*" was used in plural that then means Jesus did not carry only one sorrow and left the other ones for you to carry. But He carried our sorrows – all of them and did not leave any for us to carry. You can only limit the number of sorrows he bore for you by your faith.

The word *"carried"* is also used in the past tense, which then suggests that before you became Born Again, before the sorrow came upon you, Jesus had already carried them. That is why even when you find yourself in a sorrowful moment you are not perturbed, because Jesus carried out sorrow. On the Calvary He was announcing to us that all things worketh together for good for those that love God and to those who are called for His purpose.

It then means that those events the devil had lined up to cause sorrows to you, God will still use them, not any other one but those particular events the enemy is relying on to align themselves together and produce good news to you, so cheer up. Those events are not meant to drown you, they are allowed by God to be used as a platform to promote you. Our brother Joseph in the book of Genesis has a proper understanding of this. Those events the enemy prepared to cause him sorrows and kill his dreams were the same events that God used to fulfill his dreams.

Further the issue of grief and sorrow are issues that affect the heart and cause heart failure. The reason why when those events comes our way we don't end up having our hearts affected is because Jesus had carried our sorrows and griefs and in its place has given us Joy and hope and the peace of mind that passeth all understanding.

The third benefit of Calvary is that Jesus was striken and smitten by God for a purpose. There is a punishment meant for every sin committed. Jesus at Calvary received those strokes from God on our behalf. God shall no longer strike or smite us when we confess our sins to Him rather, He will forgive us and cleanse us from all unrighteousness.

That is why Jesus at Calvary was announcing to us that the arrow that flieth by day will neither strike us nor the pestilence that walketh in darkness, nor the destruction that wasteth at noonday smite us. While he was at Calvary He was announcing to us His followers and believers that the sun shall not smite us by day nor the moon by night. By reason of Calvary, we now have divine protection against the elemental beings and against all the arrows of the enemy. We need then not to be afraid when we hear the calamities that befall others or our neighbours, they are not meant for us and will not be our portion in Jesus name; because Jesus received them on our behalf.

The fourth benefit of Calvary is that Jesus was afflicted for our cause. Jesus had the power to reject any form of affliction. When the people came to arrest him in the Garden of Gethsemane his glory brought all of them down, but He still submitted Himself to be afflicted to fulfill God's purpose for our life.

That is why the bible refers to the affliction we experience as light affliction as in 2Cor. 4:17 – *"for our light affliction, which is but for a moment, worketh for us a far more exceeding and eternal weight of glory."*

The main afflictions have been carried by Jesus so the light affliction left for us is just for a moment and is there to help us receive eternal weight of glory.

Is the devil afflicting you now either in your body, marriage or business or through your children, in-law and extended families? Relax, Jesus is announcing to you that the little affliction you are feeling now is just for a moment and it will soon expire to achieve or bring you into a wonderful glory.

The reason the Bible said affliction will not come the second time is because when it came the first time Jesus received it and carried it on the Calvary when he nailed it to the cross to deny it the power to come the second time. The light affliction that comes more than once was not the one crucified with Jesus on the cross, the light affliction referred to are those channels that have been prepared by God to become channels to bring you into your inheritance.

The Fifth benefit of Calvary is that Jesus was wounded for our transgression, and bruised for our iniquities. Jesus carried this injury he received when he was wounded and bruised and went to Calvary. On top of the cross He showed Himself to the whole world and to devil and his agents and announced to them that concerning his followers: *"touch not mine anointed and do my prophet no harm"*. So any attack of the enemy that brings harm to us by way of wounding or bruising us is an act of disobedient to the word of the master and must be judged by the master.

That is why we should not be afraid; Jesus had warned them not to do any harm to His anointed. In the same vein Jesus also announced to His followers – *"no weapon formed against us shall prosper, any tongue that rises against us in judgment we shall condemn"* because Jesus had received all the wounds and bruises the devil intended for us.

Have you been wounded or bruised emotionally, financially or maritally? Don't worry Jesus had paid the price so no demand of any punishment should be made of you.

The sixth benefit of Calvary is that the chastisement of our peace was placed upon Him. Chastisement means to punish severely. When you go through the scripture and discover what Jesus was subjected to in order to redeem us you may even question why such punishment or level of suffering should be meted out on Him.

We now know the reason; because the chastisement of our peace was upon Him. He carried the punishment not just meant for one person but for the whole world. The number of people involved in the salvation Jesus came to give increased the level of punishment released on Him.

Severe suffering is hot for you, it is an aberration and it's contrary to the word of God. Chastisement from the devil is not for us as children of God.

The seventh benefit of Calvary was that the stripes He received and carried to the cross made provision for our healing – 1Pet. 2:24 – ***"Who his own self bare our sins in his own body on the tree, that we, being dead to sins, should live unto righteousness by whose stripes ye were healed."***

When Jesus came here on earth God anointed Him with power and he was going about doing good and healing all manner of diseases and sickness in Acts. 10:38 – ***"How God anointed Jesus of Nazareth with the Holy ghost and with power, who went about doing good and healing all that were oppressed of the devil, for God was with him."***

Since Jesus knew that once He resurrect and lives in heaven, He may not have the opportunity of physically moving from one place to another to heal people, He then allowed Himself to be scourged (that is flogged) as to have stripes resulting from the scourging. As He went to the cross, He then announced both to the whole world and the devil and his agents that by His stripes shall His people be healed anytime the devil afflicts them with sicknesses or diseases. So whatever sickness or disease that is affecting you now or a member of your family, Jesus is not interested in the name of the sickness. The name of the sickness or disease does not intimidate Jesus, He is telling us that his stripes are enough to bring the desired healing because healing is the children's (children of God) bread. So have faith and apply the stripes of Jesus to that sickness or disease. I have an assurance of faith that you must receive your healing.

The eight benefit of Calvary is that our iniquities were laid upon Him. Which means that my sins and all my iniquities have been laid upon Jesus and God has forgiven me all my sins, I have become the righteousness of God through Jesus Christ.

By what He did on the cross He became the propitiation for our sins – He was made the scapegoat because of our sins. Jesus on the cross informed us and even the devil and its agents that the bondage of sin over our lives is *"finished"*. Sin shall no longer have mastery over our bodies. But even if by mistake we sin against God, Jesus has become our advocate in heaven so if we confess our sins, God is faithful and Just to forgive us our sins and cleanse us from all unrighteousness.

It is not just forgiving us our sins, but because of Calvary, God went a step further to cleanse us from an impurity that has come in contact with our body by reason of those sins. He (God) also at Calvary provided the best and most efficacious detergent needed to cleanse us from unrighteousness using the blood of Jesus.

We are not just forgiven, but by cleansing us we come back to the righteous position Jesus brought us through His death before we sinned so that God can look upon us and resume fellowship with us because Habakkuk 1:13a says *"Thou are of purer eyes than to behold evil and canst not look on iniquity…"* God does not allow His eyes to see sin or iniquity or fellowship with sin.

The Ninth benefit of Calvary is that Jesus was brought as a Lamb to the slaughter and as a sheep before her shearers.

Jesus became our sacrificial Lamb – the Lamb of God. God in His desire to restore man back to His fellowship needed a sacrifice that is perpetual, efficacious and righteous, no person or animal qualified for the standard of God but God refused to be discouraged or allowed His eternal plan thwarted. He then provided Himself a Lamb.

In Ezekiel 18:14 – *"Behold all souls are mine; as the soul of the father, so also the soul of the son is mine. The soul that sinneth, it shall die."*

By reason of our sins against God we are supposed to die (spiritual death apart from the physical death – being separated from God forever). But Jesus went and died for us so that we shall no longer taste death. What is only left for a believer is translation from this earth to heaven. As in Heb. 2:9 – *"But we see Jesus, who was made a little lower than the angles for the suffering of death crowned with glory and honour, that he by the grace of God should taste death for every man."*

By Jesus death on the cross we have been delivered from the terror and fear of death and He also delivered us from he that has the power of death. In Heb. 2:14, 15 – *"Forasmuch then as the children are partakers of flesh and blood, he also himself likewise took part of the same, that through death he might destroy him that had the power of death, that is, the devil; and deliver them, who through fear of death were all their lifetime subject to bondage."*

We have victory over death by what Jesus did at Calvary even when the spirit of death visits us personally or our family, business or marriage, we can stand boldly to rebuke and challenge it and command it to get out of our life.

Calvary had made us better prophets with greater authority than Prophet Ezekiel. In Ezekiel chapter 37, we can by the authority received from Jesus prophesy unto every dead issue or dry bones in our business, marriage or family and expect life to come to them.

Jesus said the word I speak they are life and spirit and has given us authority to do greater work than he did. More so whatever we bind or loose in heaven is bound or loosed on earth. By his death we have assurance of salvation as written – Rom. 5:10 – *"for if, when we were enemies, we were more, being reconciled, we shall be saved by his life."*

CHAPTER SEVEN
JESUS LIFESTYLE

Jesus would have come to this world, live in a solitary place and at the time of his death may manifest himself then die. He would have still achieved His divine purpose to die and give us salvation.

He chose by divine arrangement to come to the world, live for some time, affect the lives of the people positively and finally release His life for us to have life.

Apart from affecting the lives of people positively, Jesus lived here on earth to show us the way to the father. In John 14:5-6 ***"Thomas saith unto him, Lord, we know not whither thou goest; and how can we know the way? Jesus saith unto him, I am the way, the truth and the life: no man cometh unto the father, but by me"***.

Jesus came to show us the way and also be the way; it then means there is a spiritual way to God and a physical way to God. The spiritual way to God is by way of salvation through our Lord Jesus Christ which qualifies us and gives us access to our heavenly father. The physical way to God is the physical lifestyle of Jesus you live here on earth after you have received the spiritual way to God. Life in the physical way without the spiritual way is religion and it cannot bring access to God neither can it give salvation.

On the other hand, the spiritual way without the physical way cannot guarantee ultimate salvation. The two are complementary to each other. It is like a person that gave his life such person though He has given his life to God through Jesus Christ cannot make heaven because in

Rev. 21:7, 8 – *"He that overcometh shall inherit all things; and I will be his God, and he shall be my son. But the fearful, and unbelieving, and the abominable and murderers, whoremongers, and sorcerers, and idolaters, and all liars, shall have their part in the lake which burneth with fire and brimstone: which is the second death".*

Because heaven is not meant for the sinful, there are characters that we cannot carry in heaven also there are habits that God will not and cannot condone in heaven.

Jesus recognized that it is not God's desire that the moment anybody becomes born again he dies and goes to heaven so there is need to put in place conduct (or lifestyle) that will not deny us the benefit of what Jesus did on the cross. See Ezekiel 33;12, *"Therefore, thou son of man, say unto the children of thy people, the righteousness of the righteous shall not deliver him in the day of his transgression: as for the wickedness of the wicked, he shall not fall thereby in the day that he turneth from his wickedness, neither shall the righteous be able to live for his righteousness in the that he sinneth. When I shall say to the righteous, that he shall surely live, if he trust to his own righteousness, and commit iniquity, all his righteousness shall not be remembered, but for his iniquity that he hath committed, he shall die for it".*

Jesus and God Almighty are conscious of the above scripture and desired that Jesus will not just come to the earth and die but to live a life that has a style filled with righteousness. In Hebrew 1:9 *"Thou hast loved righteousness and hated iniquity, therefore God, even thy God hath anointed thee with the oil of gladness above thy fellows"*. Jesus lived a lifestyle worthy of emulation.

Note that His lifestyle was not a lifestyle in a sinless world or a lifestyle without temptation. But he was equally tempted and tried but he did not fall to such temptation but remained focused. See Heb. 4:5 *"For we have not a high priest which cannot be touched with the feeling of our infirmities, but was in all points tempted like as we are, yet without sin"*.

While Jesus was here on earth there are some characters He exhibited that are worthy of emulation which will help us in our Christian race to live a victorious Christian life. We should note that Christianity is not a religion but it is a way of life. Religion is man seeking for a way to seek and get God's attention through sacrifice and fleshly work. While Christianity is God seeking a way to reconcile man back to Himself through Jesus Christ.

The Christianity we practice is not an embodiment of religious practices but a way of life or a life style that conform the word of God with righteousness from our business practice to our family day to day living.

Jesus lived a life that affected his followers. His followers did not only see His lifestyle but allowed the lifestyle to affect them to the extent that those people in Antioch who did not see Jesus physically saw Jesus lifestyle in their lives and called them Christians.

The purpose of stating some of the characters Jesus exhibited here on earth is for us to know them and pattern our life accordingly.

(A) HOLINESS

In Peter 2:22 we read ***"Who did no sin, neither was found in his mouth"*** Jesus lived in a world full of sin and also was tempted but He refused to commit any sin.

Jesus lived above board because the things of the world were never a priority to Him. He knew His mission, kept to it with all that He has around Him. The devil tempted Jesus with fame and power for the bible said that He showed Him all the kingdoms of the world in a moment and promised to give Him all of them if He (Jesus) will bow down and worship Him. Jesus refused the offer and overcame the temptation. Living a holy life does not mean that as a believer you will not be tempted. Most often you are tempted in the area your desire is inclined with James 1:14 – ***"But man is tempted when he is drawn away of his own lust and enticed"***.

But Jesus knew that the power He has is holy, the father that sent him is holy, so He cannot work effectively, effectively and enduring without being holy. See Exodus 15:11 – ***"Who is like unto thee O Lord, among the gods? Who is like thee, glorious in holiness, fearful in praises, doing wonders?"*** Jesus knew that for His ministry to witness the glory of God and the wonders of His hand, He must live a holy life.

In the same 1 Peter 2:22, the bible stated that Guile (deceit) was not found in His mouth. O you servant of God or believer is your life full of deceit. You cannot go far in your ministry. Have you come to a point you tell one person one thing and another person another, has a chameleon visited your mouth that you are operating with chameleon spirit? You change your word as you see different people. Definitely you are digging the grave of your ministry.

Have you come to a point that deceit of the mouth is operating in your life even when you are on the pulpit. If you don't stop now your sin will discover you. The bible said in 2 Tim. 2:19 – *"Nevertheless the foundation of God standeth sure, having this seal, the Lord knoweth them that are his. And let everyone that nameth the name of Christ depart from iniquity"*.

Jesus was also mindful of what He says. We should be careful in our all round conversation whether in our family life or business circle. Some are Christians when it comes to the things of the spirit and are carnal or unbelievers when it comes to issue of business, family and the customs of the world.

The things we say will be part of what God will use to measure the level of holiness in our life. Remember no man shall see God without holiness.

(B) <u>HUMILITY</u>

Humility may be defined as understanding my weakness or limitations and striving not to lift up myself above others. In 1 Peter 5:5 we read *"Likewise, ye younger submit yourselves unto the elder. Yeas, all of you be subject one to another and be clothed with humility. God resist the proud and giveth grace to the humble"*.

Jesus humbled Himself that is to say submitted himself to authority. Because He submitted to God's authority, He also was able to submit to human authority just to accomplish the purpose of God.

We can see this in 1Pet. 2:22-23 – *"who did no sin, neither was guile found in his mouth: who, when he was reviled, reviled not again; when he suffered, he threatened not; but committed himself to him that judgeth righteously:"*

Jesus left us an example to follow. Because He was humble, submitting to the will of God was a priority in His life and whatever he does.

Humility is not just seen when you walk or talk quietly. It is an issue of heart. It is adjudged by what you do and what you say.

Humility is not properly measured when there is a deficiency in your life or a lack in your life. When you are poor or intellectually backward you behave quietly, submissive to any instruction because of what you want to gain or achieve. May be if you are lacking, the moment money comes in and may be you purchase a car, land etc you become haughty. May be the moment you graduate from the University with a degree and you look at yourself now as an accountant, lawyer, doctor or an engineer, you become arrogant.

Look at the life of Jesus and discover that, position, fame or money never changed His humble life style despite all that he possesses. A writer stated about Jesus and said *"He agreed to talk our language, to wear our clothes, to eat our food, to breathe our air, and to endure our vile and vicious treatment."* In the epistle of Paul to the Philippians we read what God revealed to the apostle about Jesus through the Holy Spirit.

Phil. 2:5-11 – *"Let this mind be in you, which was also in Christ Jesus: who, being in the form of God, thought it not robbery to be equal of a servant, and was made in the likeness of men: and being found in fashion as a man, he humbled himself, and became obedient unto death, even the death of the cross. Wherefore God also hath highly exalted him, and given him a name which is above every name: that at the name of Jesus every knee should bow of things in heaven and things in earth, and things under the earth; and that every tongue should confess that Jesus Christ is Lord, to the Glory of God the father."*

(C) <u>COMPASSIONATE</u>

Compassion means expressing a deep feeling of love and concern for others needs and difficulties. In 1Pet. 3:8 – *"Finally, be ye all of one mind, having compassion one for another, love as brethren, be pitiful be courteous."*

The compassion of Jesus for mankind did not start here on earth, it started from heaven when He saw the spiritual and physical death man brought upon himself by reason of the sins of Adam. He really had compassion for his helplessness and that moved Him to come and die for man so that man can be reconciled back to God and regain the original position God kept for him.

When Jesus visited the tomb where Lazarus was laid in John 11:35, he wept. The weeping of Jesus was not because he was helpless to heal or raise Lazarus from the dead. That was not His problem because he knew earlier that Lazarus was dead and He was going to raise him from the dead. But what moved Jesus to weep was the helplessness and hopelessness of man at the hands of death being the resultant effect of the sin of Adam. Jesus was moved by compassion for mankind in general which resulted in his weeping and the raising of the dead. The Bible stated that Jesus loved Lazarus, loved Mary and Martha, they also loved Jesus but it was not enough to stop death or spirit of untimely death to mesmerize the family of Lazarus. It took the compassion of Jesus to heal and break the curse of untimely death in the family of Lazarus.

Some events are allowed by God to come to a certain point before he intervenes so that He will deal with the root of the problem. If Jesus had come at the time Mary and Martha sent for Him, He would only have dealt with the issue at hand and that was sickness. Jesus would have healed him without dealing with the spirit of untimely death. But when he tarried and came at the time his Father wanted it, He was able to deal once with the curses of untimely death in the family of Brother Lazarus.

Most of the miracles Jesus did were born out of His compassion for the people. Matt. 14:14 – *"And Jesus went forth, and saw a great multitude, and was moved with compassion toward them, and he healed their sick."* In Mark 8:1,2 – *"In those days the multitude being very great, and having nothing to eat, Jesus called his disciples unto him, and saith unto them I have compassion on the multitude, because they have now been with me three days and have nothing to eat."*

This led to the four thousand men fed by Jesus Christ during His ministry. In Matt. 9:36 – *"But when he saw the multitudes, he was moved with compassion on them, because they fainted, and were scattered abroad, as sheep having no shepherd."*

For your ministry to move forward know that compassion is one of the prerequisites of moving it forward. Have compassion for the people you are ministering to or about to minister to and miracles will follow.

(D) <u>GENTLENESS:</u>

Gentleness is defined as being patient and kind to others. In 2Tim. 2:24 – *"And the servant of the Lord must not strive, but be gentle unto all men, apt to teach, patient."*

Striving with people either in the ministry or in the compound where you live is not a character expected of any servant of the Lord. Sometimes it could be to show off or seen as an occasion to introduce yourself as a great man of God that has great-men-connection.

One of the qualities of Jesus was learning to be patient with people. He had an excellent way of handling and managing people.

Who could have looked at the early life of the apostles and still continue to work with them. Men whose life style was infested with ambition and strife. We saw the ambitions of James and John to sit at the left and right hand of Jesus. We also saw the ambitions of the apostles for the restoration of power to the Israelites even at the end of Jesus ministry on earth in Acts 1:6 – *"When they therefore were come together, they asked of him, saying Lord, wilt thou at this time restore again the kingdom to Israel."*

Jesus never considered the ambitions of James and John but he made them to be among the closest of his apostles. The ambitions of the people did not affect his love and purpose for them rather He was gentle and patient with their level of spiritual understanding. He still sent down the Holy Spirit to bring the required change needed in their lives to produce the required divine purpose and fulfillment of Jesus ministry.

Jesus gentleness was not only to His disciples and apostles; it was also to the heathen and government authorities. We see in Matt. 17:24, 27 – *"And when they were come to Capernaum, they that received tribute money came to Peter and said, doth not your master pay tribute?...notwithstanding, lest we should offend them, go thou to the sea, and cast an hook, and take up the fish that first cometh up; and when thou has opened his mouth, thou shalt find a piece of money, that take and give unto them for me and thee."*

Jesus became gentle to them because He does not want to offend them. As servants of the Lord gentleness is required of us and not at the slightest provocation we will flare up and release all manner of curses.

(E) <u>MEEKNESS</u>:

Meekness means yielding everything to God though you may have all power and authority at your disposal. In Ps. 22:26 – *"The meek shall eat and be satisfied. They shall praise the Lord that seek him your heart shall live for ever."*

Jesus knew the importance of meekness as a Godly character and He exhibited it. In Matt. 11:28-30 – *"Come unto me, all ye that labour and are heavy laden, and I will give you rest. Take my yoke upon you, and learn of me, for I am meek and lowly in heart and ye shall find rest unto your souls. For my yoke is easy, and my burden is light."*

Jesus when He was exhibiting this character of meekness one of the apostles who did not understand Him forbade Him but He strictly warned him so that he does not constitute a nuisance or a hindrance to the exhibition of his Godly character.

In John 13:4,5 – *"He riseth from supper, and laid aside his garments and took a towel,* **and girded himself**

after that he poureth water into a basin and began to wash the disciples's feet and to wipe them with the towel wherewith he was girded". In verse 14 of John chapter 13 – **"If I then, your Lord and master, have washed your feet; ye also ought to wash one another's feet"**.

Since meekness also required total submission to God,by yielding all Jesus did that in His suffering and death. See Isa. 53:7 – **"He was oppressed, and he was afflicted, yet he opened not his mouth: he is brought as a lamb to the slaughter, and as a sheep before her shearers is dumb, so he openeth not his mouth"**.

(F) <u>OBEDIENCE:</u>

Obedience is defined as willingness to do what God requires of you. In Deu. 13:4 – "Ye shall walk after the Lord your God, and fear him and keep his commandments, and obey his voice, and ye shall serve him and cleave unto him".

The life of Jesus was an epitome of obedient life throughout the life time of His ministry in John 4:34 we read – **"Jesus saith unto them, my meat is to do the will of Him that sent me, and to finish his work"**.

Right from onset Jesus knew He was here on earth to accomplish a divine mission and every opportunity he had, He used it to inform his hearers of his will to do the will of His father. In Luke 2:49 – **"And he said unto them (Joseph and Mary), how is it that ye sought me? Wist ye not that I must be about my father's business?"** Obedience to the work and word of God characterized His ministry. He put into practice that which He told his earthly parents. In John.15:10 – "If ye keep my commandments, ye shall abide in my love, even as I have kept my father's commandments and abide in his love".

In the last line of verse 15 of John chapter 15 – "..**For all things that I have heard of my father, I have made known unto you**".

Jesus indeed lived a life of total obedience even when His desire ran contrary to the will of God but because he was obedient He would rather submit to the will of God than his own will. We saw this in His prayer in the Garden of Gethsemane   in Luke 22:42 – "**Saying, father, if thou be willing, remove this cup from me: nevertheless, not my will, but thine be done.**

He submitted to the will of God even unto death. Not just any how death or a type of death chosen by Jesus himself but the type God the father had pre-destined. In Phil. 2:8 – "**And being found in fashion as a man, he humbled himself, and became obedient unto death, even the death of the cross**".

Are we ready to be obedient as Jesus was. Don't say He was obedient because He was God. Abraham also obeyed God when God said he should sacrifice his only beloved son Isaac, he did not consider anything but simply obeyed God. To eat the best of the land, you must be willing and obedient unto God. (Isa. 1:19).

(G) <u>THANKFULNESS:</u>

Thankfulness can be defined as expressing appreciation to God and others the way they have shown you favour or kindness. In 1 Thess. 5:8 – "**In everything give thanks: for this is the will of God in Christ Jesus concerning you**".

In 2 Thess. 2:13 – **"But we are bound to give thanks always to God for you brethren beloved of the Lord, because God hath from the beginning choose you to salvation through sanctification of the spirit and belief of the truth"**.

Jesus though was God and also on God's divine assignment remained thankful to God in the course of executing His vision and fulfillment of His ministry. During the feeding of the four thousand Jesus used prayer with thanksgiving to bring down a miracle that satisfied all the multitudes that followed Him. In Mark 8:5, 6 – **"And he asked them, how many loaves have ye? And they said, seven. And he commanded the people to sit down on the ground and he took the seven loaves, and <u>gave thanks,</u> and brake and gave to his disciples to set before them, and they did set them before the people"**.

Jesus knew what the heart of thanksgiving does to one's ministry or prayer life. The bible admonished us in Phil. 4:6 – **"Be careful for nothing but in <u>everything by prayer and supplication with thanksgiving</u> let you request be made known unto God.**

Another attribute that assisted the character of thanksgiving is contentment – to be content in whatever state or position God has placed you. Contentment means accepting whatever God provides for your life. Paul emphasizing this point stated in Phil. 4:11 – **"Not that I speak in respect of want: for I have learned in whatsoever state I am, therewith to be content"**, Godliness with contentment is great gain.

Jesus was contented with whatever position or place God kept him. With the attribute of contentment the life of thanksgiving flows naturally. Nothing is too difficult for that soul that has a lifestyle of thanksgiving in every situation.

(H) TOLERANCE

Tolerance as being patient with the weakness of others. In 1 Thess. 5:14 – **"Now we exhort you brethren, warn then that are unruly, comfort the feeble minded, <u>support the weak, be patient towards all men"</u>.**

Jesus well understood the weakness of men and knows how to encourage them rather than use their weakness to suppress or kill them. Jesus saw a weakness in Peter; the devil also saw weakness in Peter and planned to use it to destroy Peter in his ministry but Jesus not only tolerated his weakness at that time went further to pray for Peter so that Peter's ministry will not be limited by devil's schemes.

In Luke 22:31, 32 – **"And the Lord said Simon, Simon, behold Satan hath desired to have you, that he may sift you as wheat. But I have prayed for thee, that thy faith fail not: and when thou are converted, strengthen thy brethren".** The only way we can learn to tolerate others easily is when we understand that we do not operate at the same level, we do not grow at the same level and all that we have or acquired was given to us by God. Moreover we should realize we are not yet perfect. Paul say in his epistle I have not apprehended ..

Tolerance is like given the other person a chance to grow at his own pace without unnecessary interference from us. In a situation where there are things in that person we cannot tolerate or live with either for a short time or long time, we can follow the example of Jesus who prayed for Peter and also commanded him to do likewise to others.

Are you strong now, take some little time to pray and strengthen the person you cannot tolerate.

Jesus also exhibited another high level of tolerance towards Peter and Judas Iscariot. Right from the beginning of his ministry, Jesus knew that somebody would deny him and the other person betray him, and they were all going to be members of his apostleship. Inspite of this knowledge, Jesus accommodated them in his ministry and even allowed them to partake in the breaking of bread which is a covenant meal.

In Luke 22:21, 22 We read – **"Behold, the hand of him that betrayed me is with me on the table. And truly the son of man goeth, as it was determined. But woe unto that man by whom he is betrayed"**.

Today if we see a brother or sister doing or saying things against us. Whether it is true or not, if we have authority as senior minister or pastor, it is either we render him or her redundant in the ministry or sack him or transfer him to a place where the best option left for him will be to resign. Jesus tolerated both the righteous and the sinners in order to ensure that they make heaven.

(I) <u>LOVE</u>
Jesus is an embodiment of love like the father. Compassion has no basis without love. Love is the tonic that facilitates compassion when you look at the chapter on love. This love gave birth to kindness which is also another character Jesus exhibited.

The watchword of Jesus is He does what He saw His father does. In John 3:16 – **"For God so loved the world, that he gave his only begotten son, that whosoever believeth in him should not perish, but have everlasting life"**.

The love Jesus had stemmed from the love His father also had for him and for mankind. Love begat love, it was this love that made Jesus to accept to die on the cross for mankind. In John 15:13 – **"Greater love hath no man than this, that a man lay down his life for his friends".** The laying down of life by Jesus is a great manifestation of love He has for us.

It is the same love that propels Jesus to enter into the ministry of intercession for the saints after his death and resurrection. Heb. 7:25 – **"Wherefore he is able also to save them to the uttermost that come unto God by him seeing he ever liveth to make intercession for them.** The evidence of love in the life of Jesus that he saves and continues to pray for the saved, so that they do not miss heaven. Also during the time of Jesus ministry on earth He ministered spiritual things unto the people. He also ministered material things like food to the people. The love of Jesus was seen in His love for God the father, His disciples, little children, certain close friends like Lazarus, Mary and Martha.

In 1 Cor. 13:13 – **"And now abideth faith, hope, charity (love) these three, but the greatest of these is charity (love)".** You may speak in tongues and exhibit all the gifts of the Holy Spirit but if one of the fruit of the Holy Spirit called love is not there you are nothing before God. See 1 Cor. 13:2,3 – **"And though I have the gift of prophecy, and understand all mysteries, and all knowledge, and though I have all faith, so that I could remove mountains, and I have not charity (love), I am nothing. And though I bestow all my goods to feed the poor, and though I give my body to be burned, and have not charity (love), it profiteth me nothing".**

(J) <u>FORGIVENESS:</u>

Forgiveness as a character has been defined as overlooking a wrong that was done unto you.

In Colossians 3:13 – **"Forbearing one another, and forgiving one another, if any man have a quarrel against any: even as Christ forgave you, so also do ye".**

Forgiveness is a Godly character that is also tied to our salvation. We received salvation because God forgave us our sins and commanded us to forgive others as He has forgiven us with a consequence of refusing to forgive us when we don't forgive others. In Matt. 6:14, 15 - **"For if ye forgive men their trespasses your heavenly father will also forgive you: but if ye forgave not men their trespasses, neither will your father forgive your trespasses".**

During the earthly ministry of Jesus he informed his audience that He has power to forgive sins and He indeed forgave people their sins. In Matt. 9:2, 6 We read – **"And behold they brought to him a man sick of the palsy, lying on a bed: and Jesus seeing their faith said unto the sick of the palsy, son be of good cheer, thy sins be forgiven thee.. But that ye may know that the son of man hath power on earth to forgive sins. (Then saith to the sick of the palsy) Arise, take up thy bed, and go unto thine house."**

Jesus does not love sin and He does not condone sins but once He sees the faith on the heart of the person to receive forgiveness from him, He gives out the forgiveness. The woman caught in adultery and Mary Magdalene received His forgiveness.

Jesus also extended His hand of forgiveness to Peter after Peter denies Him three times. He not only forgave Peter but

He also re-instated Peter to His position of leadership and fellowship with God.

There were so many Godly characters Jesus exhibited which testified His lifestyle that this book may not be able to record all. Only just a few examples to encourage and to inform us that Jesus left good examples for us to follow.

CHAPTER EIGHT

THE MYSTERY IN THE BODY AND BLOOD OF JESUS

In the gospel according to John 6:53-**58 "Then Jesus said unto them, verily, verily I say unto you, except ye eat the flesh of the son of man and drink his blood, ye have no life in you. Whoso eateth my flesh, and drinketh my blood, hath eternal life, and I will raise up at the last day. For my flesh is meat indeed and my blood is drink indeed. He that eaten my flesh and drinketh my blood dwelleth in me and I in him. As the living father hath sent me, and I live by the father: so he that eateth me, even he shall live by me. This is that bread which came down from heaven: not as your fathers did eat manna, and are dead: he that eateth of this bread shall live forever".**

One of the reasons why Jesus came to die was to give us life that is why He said I am the resurrection and life. Every man born by woman had Adam's sin in his life and are serving death sentence imposed upon him by reason of Adam's sin. But when Jesus came He said in John 10:10b .. "I am come that they might have life and that they have it more abundantly".

Now in John Chapter 6 Jesus said except a man eats His flesh and drinks His blood He cannot have that life Jesus came to bring to us. He went further that as you partake in the flesh and blood of Jesus you will not just have life but you will have eternal life and He will raise you up on the last day.

We then discovered that your partaking in the flesh and blood of Jesus is a prerequisite for your obtaining and receiving eternal life. Not only that, it also has to do with rapture that the second coming of our Lord Jesus Christ because it will qualify you to be raised by Jesus on the last day.

The flesh and blood of Jesus is quite relevant to the life of the Christian who has given his or her life to Jesus. Your partaking in the eating and drinking of the flesh and blood of Jesus will only have meaning after you have first of all given your life to Him, thereafter your eternal life and going to heaven are guaranteed.

Note that the message was to Christ followers, his disciples. It is a message that can only be understood by those who have already given their lives to Jesus. Those that are not born again lack the spiritual understanding what Jesus meant by His flesh and His blood.

There is indeed a mystery behind this message of eating and drinking of the flesh and blood of Jesus which we must depend upon the Holy Spirit to bring to our own understanding. But if throughout our stay on earth we did not come to that understanding, the best thing to do is to walk by faith and do as we have been commanded to do.

Looking at verse 58 of John chapter 6 Jesus described Himself as that bread from heaven. There is indeed a relationship between the flesh of Jesus and bread. He is described as the bread of life.

We read in John 6:47-52 as followers "Verily, verily I say unto you, he that believeth on me hath everlasting life. I am that bread of life. Your fathers did eat manner in the wilderness and are dead. This is the bread which cometh down from heaven: if any man eats of this bread, he shall live forever: and the <u>bread that I will give is my flesh</u> which I will give for the life of the world"

Sometimes we find it difficult to believe some of Jesus sayings. That is why it is important that we must depend upon the Holy Spirit to give us proper understanding on messages like this. Jesus said in John 16:12, 13 "I have yet many things to say unto you, but ye cannot bear them now. Howbeit when he the spirit of truth, is come, he will guide you into all truth: for he shall not speak of himself; but whatsoever he shall hear, that shall he speak: and he will shew things to come".

So if you don't rely upon the Holy Spirit you may not understand like the Jews and start asking some funny questions. In John 6:52 "The Jews therefore strove among themselves, saying how can this man give us his flesh to eat?.

It was also not only the Jews, even the disciples that did not seek the face of the Holy Spirit also lacked the understanding and murmured in John 6:60, 61 "Many therefore of his disciples, when they had heard this, said this is an hard saying, who can hear it? When knew in himself that his disciples murmured at it, he said unto them, doth this offend you?.

THE RELATIONSHIP BETWEEN THE FLESH AND THE BREAD, THE BLOOD AND THE WINE

We read in John 6:50, 51 "This is the bread which cometh down from heaven, that a man may eat thereof and not die. I am the living bread which came down from heaven. If any man eats of this bread, he shall live forever and the bread that I will give is my flesh, which I will give for the life of the world".

It is indeed obvious from the above text that there is a relationship between flesh and the bread and between the blood and the wine.

Before we go further into the mysteries of flesh and blood in relationship to the breaking of bread and drinking of wine, we need to look through the scriptures and discover that the issue of bread and wine has been there before Jesus came physically on earth. The major difference being that Jesus gave His own flesh and the mystery behind it is that this flesh became the living bread that came from heaven and today He declares to everybody that He is the bread of life.

The issue of bread and wine is not just New Testament doctrine that was instituted by Jesus. It has been there and has from time to time been used by God through His ministers to administer to the people. The difference still remains that those who eat this bread and wine still die but those who partake in this living bread, death has no dominion over their life. What they experience is translation to the kingdom of God in heaven.

During the lifetime of Abraham the father of faith, he received this bread and wine from a priest of God called Melchizedek. In Gen. 14:18-20 –We read "and Melchizedek king of Salem brought forth bread and wine he was the priest of the most high God, possessor of heaven and earth. And he gave him tithes of all".

Melchizedek was the prophet of God who administered the bread and wine to Abraham but did not have the spiritual understanding of it.

That is to say that the issue of bread and wine is an act that heaven initiated and occasionally allowed those who have qualified spiritually to partake in it.

Though that bread and wine were given to Abraham for spiritual refreshment and consolation it does not give eternal life because is not the bread of life.

Abraham also recognized the spiritual significance of the bread and wine Melchizedek gave him, that prompted him to pay the first tithe ever paid to Melchizedek. That also opened his eye to understanding the spiritual superiority of Melchizedek and submitted to the blessings of Melchizedek. We can read this in Heb. 7:1, 4, 7 – "For this Melchizedek, king of Salem, priest of the most High God, who met Abraham.. Now consider how great this man was, unto whom even the patriarch Abraham gave the tenth of the spoils... And without all contradiction the less is blessed of the better".

The next time we heard about the flesh and the unleavened bread was during the time the Israelites were to leave Egypt for the promised land in Exo. 12:3, 8 "Speak ye unto all the congregation of Israel saying, in the tenth day of this month they shall take to them every man a lamb according to the house of their fathers a lamb for a house. And they shall eat the flesh in that night, roast with fire, and unleavened bread, and with bitter herbs they shall eat it".

This is the incident that led to the establishment of Passover by God for the Israelites. It is not only that they observed it for only that day but God commanded that the feast of Passover should be kept from one generation to another generation. In Exo. 12:11 – We read "And thus shall ye eat it, with your lions guirded, your shoes on your feet, and your staff in your hand; and ye shall eat it in haste. It is the LORD'S Passover.

Further in Exodus 12:14 – "And this day shall be unto you for a memorial, and ye shall keep it a feast to the Lord throughout your generations, ye shall keep it a feast by an ordinance forever".

Here we saw the lamb being involved and the Bible said Jesus was the lamb of God sacrificed for our own sake and He said His flesh is the bread of life.

We also see the elements of flesh and bread being involved in this ordinance before Jesus came to sacrifice his own flesh and commanded us to partake in the eating of his flesh and drinking of his blood.

We saw in this first Passover that the blood of the lamb was to be painted on the door post of all the Israelites as to avoid being visited by the Angel of death (or spirit of destruction). In Exodus 12:13 – "And the blood shall be to you for a token upon the houses where ye are; and when I see the blood, I will pass over you, and the plague shall not be upon you to destroy, when I smite the land of Egypt".

While in the New Testament the blood is still used for overcoming the devil and it's kingdom in Rev. 12:11a – "and they overcame him by the blood of the lamb".

In the first Passover the blood was as a token upon their houses because God was still living in houses made by human hands but now the blood is not required as a token upon the houses but for us to drink it, it is now a token for our body now God does not live in a house made with hand. Acts 7:48 – "Howbeit the Most High dweleth not in temples made with hands, as saith the prophet". But our body has become the temple or dwelling place of God. In 1 Cor. 3:16 -"Know ye not that ye are the temple of God and that the spirit of God dwelleth in you?".

Building is no longer God's focus, it is you that is the focus of God. So the blood of the lamb is needed as a token in your own body. It is the body that Jesus is interested in, it is the body that Jesus knocks at to enter and have his fullness to dwell in it. Rev. 3:20 – "Behold, I stand at the door , and knock: if any man hear my voice, and open the door, I will come in to him and will sup with him, and he with me.

THE PASSOVER
The Passover became an institutionalized ceremony from one generation to another. It is the same event of eating the flesh, the bread and sprinkling of the blood. The Lord's Passover that started in Egypt became a continuous occasion for breaking of bread by the Israelites with one another and also with God. In Exodus 12:21,

27 – ""Then Moses called for all the elders of Israel, and said unto them, draw out and take you a lamb according to your families, and kill the Passover .That ye shall say, it is the sacrifice of the LORD'S Passover, who passed over the houses of the children of Israel in Egypt, when he smote the Egyptians, and delivered our houses. And the people bowed the head and worshipped".

From this time God declared that it has to be observed from generation to generation Exodus 12:24 – "And ye shall observe this thing for in an ordinance to thee and to thy sons forever".

This Passover indeed have been observed from one generation to other. In the time of Joshua it was observed for the first time in the promised land Joshua 5:10 –"and the children of Israel encamped in Gilgal and kept the Passover on the fourteenth day of the month at even in the plains of Jericho".

In the time of Josiah it was also observed in 2 Kings 23:21-22 – "And the king commanded all the people saying, keep the Passover unto the Lord your God, as it is written in the book of this covenant, surely there was not holden such a Passover from the days of the judges that judges Israel, nor in all the days of the kings of Israel nor of the kings of Judah"

It was also observed in Hezekiah's reign see 2 Chron.30:2 The returning remnant back to Israel from the captivity also observed the Passover See Ezra 6:19 – "And the children of the captivity kept the Passover upon the fourteenth day of the first month".

The feast of Passover did not end with the Old Testament it continued into the New Testament even our Lord Jesus at the age of twelve with His parents observed this great feast Luke 2:41, 42 – "Now his parents went to Jerusalem every year at the feast of the Passover. And when he was twelve years old, they went up to Jerusalem after the custom of the feast".

The feast of Passover did not end with Jesus when His parents took Him to Jerusalem. Even during His ministry He continued to observed the Passover. It was during the feast of the Passover that He entered the temple to cleanse it. John 2:13, 14 – " And the Jew's Passover was at hand, and Jesus went up to Jerusalem, and found in the temple those that sold oxen and sheep and doves, and the changer of money sitting.."

It was also during the feast of Passover that great multitude came to Jesus which led to the feeding of five thousand men. See John 6:4-5. It was also during the feast of Passover that Jesus raised Lazarus from the dead John 11:55.

The last supper Jesus had with His apostles was also during the feast of Passover Matt. 26:17-19 – Now the first day of the feast of unleavened bread the disciples came to Jesus, saying unto him, where wilt thou that we prepare for thee to eat the Passover. And he said, go into the city to such a man, and say unto him, the master saith, my time is at hand; I will keep the Passover at thy house with my disciples. And the disciples did as Jesus had appointed them, and they made ready the Passover".

There was something Jesus did in this particular Passover, it was no longer the same Passover that they have hitherto observed. What did he do?. Matt. 26:26 – 28 – "And as they were eating, Jesus took bread and blessed it, and brake it and gave it to the disciples, and said, take eat, this is my body. And he took the cup and gave thanks, and gave it to them saying drink ye all of it. For this is my blood of the New Testament, which is shed for many for the remission of sins."

Jesus in this last supper laid a New foundation for the feast of Passover. The Passover for the New Testament is no longer eating animal flesh and bread but is now breaking of bread which represents the body of Jesus and drinking the wine which represents the blood of Jesus. We are expected to work in the new order that Jesus had established. Any religion or organization that still slaughters animal and command the members to eat the flesh and drink the blood is occultic. It is sacrifice unto the devil.

When Jesus finished the feast of Passover with the apostles according to the new order He had established, he also gave us a command as in Luke 22:19 – "And he took bread and gave thanks, and brake it, and gave unto them saying. This is my body which is given for you: <u>this do in remembrance of me</u>".

Jesus re-emphasized that it is a practice that must continue from one generation to another.

Jesus also got involved in the same braking of bread after His resurrection. In Luke 24:30, 31 – "And it came to pass, as he sat at meat with them, he took bread, and blessed it and brake and gave to them. And their eyes were opened, and they knew him, and he vanished out of their sight".

Apart from the breaking of bread or eating of the flesh during the Passover, the history of Israelites in their dealings with God had been associated with bread.

In the time of their journey in the wilderness God threw down bread from heaven which the Israelites called manna. It has the semblance of flesh and also a semblance of bread. See Exodus 16:12-15 – "I have heard the murmuring of the children of Israel speak unto them saying, at even ye shall eat flesh, and in the morning ye shall be filled with bread, and ye shall know that I am the LORD your God. And it came to pass, that at even the quails came up, and covered the camp: and in the morning the dew lay a small round thing, as small as the hoar frost on the ground. And when the children of Israel saw it, they said one to another, it is manna: for they wist not what was. And Moses said unto them. This is the bread which the Lord hath given you to eat".

John 6:32, 33 – " Then Jesus said unto them, verily verily, I say unto you, Moses gave you not that bread from heaven, but my father giveth you the true bread from heaven. For the bread of God is he which cometh down from heaven, but my father giveth you the true bread from heaven". The issue of bread became a Spiritual constitutional matter to the people of Israel that it became one of the properties that must be in the tabernacle God asked Moses to build. In Heb. 9:2 – "For there was a tabernacle made the first, wherein was the candlestick, and the table, and the shew bread; which is called the sanctuary.

The sanctuary became a place for the shew bread not just for show but for the Israelites to dine with God spiritually. Apart from the shew bread, a representative of the manna described above was in tabernacle. Heb. 9:4 "Which had the golden censer, and the ark of the covenant overlaid roundabout with gold, wherein was the golden pot that had manna, and Aaron's rod that budded, and the tables of the covenant.

1. THE EFFECTS OR RESULTS OF THE BODY (BREAD) AND THE BLOOD (WINE)

Like I said earlier Jesus turned the Passover into a feast of breaking of bread that represents his body and drinking of wine that represents his blood. This event is not just ordinary because there are things God used the occasion to achieve in the life of his people. Some of these results can be mentioned as follows.

(a)   The feast of breaking bread is no longer a yearly event as

> Was the case in the time of the parents of Jesus Christ Luke 2:41 – "Now his parents went to Jerusalem every year at the feast of the Passover". When Jesus broke the bread during the last supper it did not take one year before he broke bread again with two of his disciples on their way to Emmaus.

Luke 24:13- 31 Jesus intends that you can be partaking in it as you may desire.

(b)   When the Passover was officially instituted, it was meant to celebrate and remember how God delivered the Israelites from the hands of the Egyptians Exodus 12:26, 27 – " And it shall come to pass, when your children shall say unto you, what mean ye by this service? That ye shall say, it is the sacrifice of the LORD'S Passover, who passed over the houses of the children of Israel in Egypt, when he smote the Egyptians, and delivered our houses. And the people bowed thy head and worshipped".

But now Jesus said we should break bread for his own remembrance. Luke 22:19 Jesus for what he did on the cross and what He is still doing in heaven interceding for us, deserve to be remembered by us. Moreover the death of Jesus on the cross had a universal effect more than the deliverance of only one nation. So let us break bread having in mind what Jesus did by dying for us and continue to pray for us in heaven.

(c)   The Passover of the Old Testament only brought deliverance to the people. It then means the people will only see the acts of God without having proper understanding about who God is. But the Passover Jesus organized has the ability to open the eyes of people spiritually so that they will not only see what God did for us through Jesus, they can as well have a spiritual understanding about who God is. The spiritual eyes of two of his disciples were opened when they partook in the breaking of bread by Jesus Luke 24:30, 31 – " And it came to pass, as he sat at meat with them, he took bread, and blessed it, and brake and gave to them. And <u>their eyes were opened and they knew him,</u> and he vanished out of their sight".

(d)   Jesus did not break the old order or command that this celebration should be from generation to generation when He said do it in remembrance of me. It then implies that it is still an event that must be observed continually from one generation to another generation, Paul writing in the same vein told all the believers in 1 Cor. 11:23-26 – "For I have received of the Lord that which also I delivered unto you, that the Lord Jesus, the same night which he was betrayed, took bread: And when he had given thanks, he brake it and said, take, eat: this is my body which is broken for you: this do in remembrance of me .. for as often as ye eat this bread, and this cup, ye do shew the Lord's death till he come".

(e)   From the scripture we discovered that Jesus did not turn His disciples to cannibals by giving them his physical body to eat, neither did they carry his body when he died and shared it and ate it just as the soldiers shared his garment. But Jesus gave them physical bread and physical wine to eat and drink and believe that the bread is His body and the wine is His blood.
That has to do with our faith life. He was working on our faith to bring it to the level we can work with God. By simply believing every word that proceeds from the mouth of God.

Moreover if we have found it difficult to believe that the bread we eat is Jesus body we will equally find it difficult to believe that we have received salvation by simply believing in our heart and confessing with our mouth. We will find it difficult to believe that, that simply alter call we answered have brought salvation unto us and our spirit has been transformed. Jesus did it to help us with God kind of faith that will help us to do greater things than He did.

(f)   Another result of the breaking of bread and drinking of wine is as stated in John 6:54 – "Whoso eateth my flesh, and drinketh my blood, hath eternal life; and I will raise him up at the last day".

One of the benefits of partaking in the breaking of bread worthily is that eternal life from Jesus is guaranteed and on the last day whether you are dead or alive Jesus will definitely raise you up to partake in the rapture that will soon take place.

(g)   There is also the indwelling presence of Jesus in our lives when we partake in the bread. John 6:56 says – "He that eateth my flesh, and drinketh my blood, dwelleth in me, and I in him". We need the dwelling in of our Lord Jesus that is when we can boldly say that He that is in me is greater than he that is in the world.

(h)   In John 6:57 – "As the living father hath sent me, and I live by the father: so he that eateth me, even he shall live by me". Our lives are now centered around Jesus. All that we do now is to have Jesus as our main focus because his presence in our life gives us the grace to live for Him. In Phil. 1:21 – "For to me to live is Christ and to die is gain". Your life is now regulated by the word of Christ, the breaking of bread will give you the enablement to live by him and for him.

2. **THE NEGATIVE IMPACT RESULTS OF PARTAKING IN THE BRAKING OF BREAD**

Just as the partaking in the breaking of bread has some positive benefits, it also has some negative effect, all depends upon the individual. The negative effects could be seen in 1 Cor. 11:29- 30, 34 – "For he that eateth and drinketh unworthily eateth damnation to himself, not discerning the Lord's body. For this cause many are weak and sickly among you, and many sleep. And if any man hunger, let him eat at home that ye come, not together unto condemnation.

Unworthy could mean eating the body of Christ as an unbeliever or as unrepented Christian, habouring malice or sin of unforgiveness while partaking in the body of Christ.

The consequences of eating the body of Christ or breaking of bread unworthy are being mentioned below as follows:

(a) The first negative effect is that the person is damned – he has made his life a doom. It becomes a miserable life. It is important that we make sure that we don't partake in the breaking of bread unworthy so that our life shall not be a life full of sorrow.

(b) Another negative effect is sickness. Those who have been healthy by reason of partaking in the breaking of bread unworthy have become sick. Those who refuse to ask for forgiveness of their sins, who know that they are not worthy but just to please others or show that they are still holy have gone to partake in the breaking of bread and thereafter attracted sickness unto themselves.

(c)   Some have remained spiritually weak as a result of partaking in the breaking of bread unworthy. No matter how many convention and conferences they have attended, their spiritual life is generally weak. Only confess your sins, partake in the breaking of bread worthily you will then receive spiritual revival.

(d)   There are people who also have died as a result of partaking in the breaking of break unworthy. The bible said "may sleep". God is not happy when his people die as a result of partaking in an event that would have brought glory to Him. God accepted us to live and fulfill the number of our days on earth in glory to his name, not to die untimely.

(e)   Some have also received condemnation as a result of unworthy participation in the breaking of bread.

The only way to avoid any of this negative result coming to us is to do as the scripture said in 1 Cor. 11:31-34 – "For if we would judge ourselves, we should not be judged. But when we are judged, we are chastened of the Lord, that we should not be condemned with the world. Wherefore, my brethren, when ye come together to eat, tarry one for another. And if any man hungry, let him eat at home; that ye come not together unto condemnation..".

WHAT IT MEANS TO PARTAKE IN AN UNWORTHY MANNER

There are ways one can partake in the breaking of bread unworthily which rather than attracts blessing associated with breaking of breaking of bread attracts curses such as in 1 Cor. 11:18 - 32

(1) Take the Lord's supper in envying and strife – 1 Cor. 11:18

(2) Take it to commemorate a mere historical fact, as the Jews celebrated the Passover – verse 19

(3) Take it in surfeiting and drunkenness 21 – 22

(4) Take it in irreverence to God and his church – verse 22

(5) Take it disrespect to the poor and needy – verse 22

(6) Take it in unbelief, not realizing its true significance, and not discerning the Lord's body and blood to receive the benefits by faith – verse 27 – 30

(7) Take it as an unsaved man with sin in his life and without making proper confession and acknowledgment of personal needs – verse 27 – 30

(8) Take it without judging self so as to escape chastening from God – verse 31 – 32.

It is now left for you to decide whether to receive the blessings or attract the curses but know that it is compulsory that you must partake in the breaking of bread but before you do it allow the word of God in 1 Cor.11;27 – 28 to guide you as stated – "Wherefore whosoever shall eat this bread, and drink this cup of the Lord, unworthily shall be guilty of the body and blood of the Lord. But let a man examine himself, and so let him eat of that bread, and drink that cup".

CHAPTER NINE

THE BENEFIT OF JESUS ADVENT

The coming of Jesus is a blessing to human race particularly with Christian believers. There are blessings God prepared and kept for us and these blessings are attached to His coming. God said in Jeremiah 29:11. – "For I know the thoughts that I think toward you, saith the Lord, thoughts of peace, and not of evil, to give you an expected end.

Furthermore in 2 Peter 1:3 we read – "According as his divine power hath given unto us all things that pertain unto life and godliness, through the knowledge of him that hath called us to glory and virtue".

In this chapter we are going to briefly look at some of the blessings attached to the salvation that Jesus brought for us. For everyone that has followed Jesus has a concern for what profit or reward is awaiting him.

The first apostles were concerned about personal reward in view of their discipleship. In the words of Peter in Mark 10:28-30 – "Then Peter began to say unto him, we have left all, and have followed thee. And Jesus answered and said, verily I say unto you, there is no man that left house, or brethren or sisters, or father or mother, or wife, or children, or lands for my sake and the gospels, but he shall receive an hundred fold now in this time houses, and brethren, and sisters and mothers, and children, and land, with persecutions, and in the world to come eternal life".

Further in 1 Cor. 15:58 We read – "Therefore, my beloved brethren, be ye steadfast, unmovable, always abounding in the work of the Lord, for as much as ye know that your labour is not in vain in the Lord."

Blessings of God are there for you as you follow Jesus and work for him. Jesus coming brought positive results to the believers and these positive results are what we call blessings:

(a)   **<u>SALVATION</u>**
In 2 Tim. 2:10 – "Therefore I endure all things for the elects sakes that they may also obtain the salvation which is in Christ Jesus with eternal glory."
There is a salvation that is in Christ Jesus and it is only when you have received Christ into your life and abide in Him continuously that you will have this salvation.

Salvation is freedom and deliverance from the sin of Adam which all that were born into the world are partakers of that sin. The law was meant to help man overcome the sin of the first man but it had a short coming that made it compulsory that Jesus must come.

Since Jesus came over 2,000 years ago all those that have believed in Him or received him have also received salvation that is in Christ Jesus.

(b)   **<u>ETERNAL LIFE</u>**
We read in John 5:11 – "And this is the record, that God hath given to us eternal life, and this life is in his son".

Beyond this life here on earth there is another life. And that life will commence after death and after judgment as in Heb. 9:27 – "And as it is appointed unto men once to die but this the judgment".

And also in Rev. 20:12, 15 – "And I saw the dead, small and great, stand before God; and the books were opened: and another book was opened, which is the book of life and dead were judged out of those things which were written in the books, according to their works…. And whosoever was not found written in the book of life was cast into the lake of fire."

Jesus came so that we can have eternal life. This is the life we shall live after death and will be guaranteed in the name of God. A life that shall be blissful in heaven. Those who accept Jesus and endure till the end shall have eternal life.

(c) **<u>SONSHIP</u>**
We read in John 1:12 – "But as many as received him, to them gave he power to become the sons of God, even to them that believe in his name".

The sins of Adam separated us from God and made us stranger to God but the coming of our Lord Jesus Christ reconciled us back to God and has given us the position of sonship in the kingdom of God. Eph. 2:19 – "Now therefore ye are no more strangers and foreigner, but fellow citizens with the saints, and of the house of God".
It then means all the right that accrues to a son in a family or household is now in your possession.

Jesus has earned for us a position in God's household, we shall no longer be treated as aliens, we have also received the spirit of sonship, now we are members of God's family. In Gal. 3:26 We read – "For ye are all the children of God by faith in Christ Jesus".

(d) **<u>NEW CREATION</u>**
In 2 Cor. 5:17, 18 – "Therefore if any man be in Christ, he is a new creature: old things are passed away, behold, all things are become new. And all things are of God hath reconciled us to himself by Jesus Christ and hath given to us the ministry of reconciliation".

The newness of life comes upon us the moment we receive Jesus into our life. This newness of life continues to expand and moves towards perfection or acquiring the divine nature of God as we continue to abide in Christ.

The new creation is that power in our innerself that helps us not to conform to the standards of the world rather continues to renew our mind in accordance with the word of God.

New creation changes our life view and gives us a new world view. Where we become more mindful of the things above rather than on the things below. Our service towards God without murmuring or grumbling.

(e)   **<u>YOU RECEIVE REST</u>**
We read in Matt. 11:28-30 – "Come unto me all ye that labour and are heavy laden, and I will give you rest. Take my yoke upon you, and learn of me for I am meek and lowly in heart: and ye shall find rest unto your souls. For my yoke is easy, and my burden is light".

Since the fall of man (because of the sins of Adam) man has been laboring to survive. The burden on man to survive has indeed been rightly described as heavy load and some have died under this yoke.

But the coming of Jesus brought rest to us. It does not mean laziness, idleness but a situation where you work a little and eat much, or where you eat the fruit of your hand. The first advent of Jesus also brought rest to our soul. Prior to this, the souls of men have indeed been in captivity to the devil except those that through the power of God liberate their soul by the observance of the laws of God.

(f)   **<u>HEALING AND DIVINE HEALTH</u>**

We read in 1 Peter 2:24 – "Who his own self bare our sins in his own body on the tree, that we being dead to sins, should live unto righteousness: by whose stripes ye were healed".

The coming of Jesus also brought provision for healing for the believers. As a believer, part of the blessings associated with Jesus' coming is the healing it provided, Jesus salvation message includes healing. In acts 10:38 We read – "How God anointed Jesus of Nazareth with the Holy Ghost and with power: who went about doing good, and healing all that were oppressed of the devil, for God was with him." No matter the nature of sickness or oppression from the devil, Jesus has provided the healing; you only need to appropriate it to your situation.

Apart from healing, the coming of Jesus also makes provision for divine health. In 3 John 2 We read – "Beloved, I wish above all things that thou mayest prosper and be in health, even as thy soul prospereth".

God had made it that you can stay from month to month, year to year and sickness will not have dominion over your life or attack you. It is yours receive it.

(g)   **<u>ABUNDANCE</u>**
In the past, old Christians believed that living in abundance is a sign of carnality. The level of your poverty or haggard look signifies your level of spirituality. But today we know from the scripture that it is not the true position. Money is not evil rather it answereth all things but is the love of money that is evil.

Jesus coming made provision for abundance and there are several scriptures that support it both in the Old Testament and New Testament for e.g Jeremiah. 29:11, 2 Peter 1:3, 3 John 2, etc.

In John 10:10 – "The thief cometh not but for to steal, and to kill and to destroy: I am come that they might have life, and that they might have it more abundantly".

Jesus knew that people ought to be prospering all the time, but sometimes the thief comes to steal from them, so he came that people should have life in abundance thereby destroying the power of the devil stealing from what God had given us.

(h)   <u>**NO CONDEMNATION**</u>

In Rom. 8:1 – "There is therefore now no condemnation to them which are in Christ Jesus, who walk not after the flesh, but after the spirit".

The issue of condemnation by the devil had been a weapon he has been using against the elect both in the Old Testament and New Testament Rev. 12:10 – "And I heard a loud voice saying in heaven now is come salvation, and strength and the kingdom of our God, and the power of His Christ: for the accuser of our brethren is cast down, which accused them before our God day and night".

The coming of our Lord Jesus has removed the condemnation of the devil against the believers. The blessings of no condemnation came with some qualifications, in essence it is only available to those who are in Christ Jesus but do not walk after the flesh, but after the spirit.

Don't allow the devil to hold you down with guilty conscience because of what you have done wrong in the past which you have confessed before God and have received forgiveness through the blood of Jesus.

(i) **<u>FREEDOM FROM THE LAW OF SIN AND DEATH</u>**
Rom. 8:2 – For the law of the spirit of life in Christ Jesus hath made me free from the law of sin and death."

The fall of man made sin to have dominion over man and sin brought death into the life of man because sin is the sting of death, without sin death does not have power over man.

When Jesus came he knew the only way man can be free from the power of death is to deal with sin so that man can be free from sin and death. The coming of Jesus brought freedom to believers from the law of sin and death. What it then means is that if in the past you fall into sin, automatically the judgment of death will come but now because of the freedom from the law of sin and death believers who sin do not have instant judgment as a way of punishment. God gives them the opportunity to confess and repent from their sins.

(j) **<u>SEATED ABOVE PRINCIPALITIES</u>**
The combined effect of these two scriptures made us to understand that we are sitting above all the powers of darkness and their agent. In Eph. 1:20, 21 We read - "Which he wrought in Christ, when he raised him from the dead, and set him at his own right hand in the heavenly places, far above all principalities, the power, and might, and dominion, and every name that is named, not only in this world, but also in that which is to come".

In Eph. 2:6 – "And raised us up together, and made us sit together in heavenly places in Christ Jesus". These scripture confirmed that the devil and his cohorts do not have dominion or authority over the lives of believers that is why Jesus talked about the power He has given to us over them Luke 10:19 – "Behold, I give unto you power to read on serpents and scorpions, and over all the power of the enemy: and nothing shall be any means hurt you".

We don't live our life in fear over that which we have been given power to dominate. We are above the devil and his agents.

(k) **<u>THE LOVE OF GOD</u>**
In John 3:16 – "For God so loved the world, that he gave his only begotten son, that whosoever believeth in him should not perish but have everlasting life".

God loveth the world, He does not want anybody to perish so God manifested the love He has for the world by sending His only begotten son to come and die for mankind. Though Jesus has died for all but it is still left for those who recognized what God did through Jesus Christ and receive it into their life that will actually experience this love of God.

The coming of Jesus has made it possible that believers in Christ Jesus do not perish but have everlasting life.

Jesus became a bridge that restored the original love that God had for the entire world. In order to partake in this great love of God He had for the entire world you need to be born again and abide in Christ forever.

(l) **<u>BAPTISM OF THE HOLY GHOST</u>**
It is indeed a great privilege to have Jesus in your life and at the same time have the Holy Ghost in your life.

We read in John 7:38, 39 – "He that believeth on me, as the scripture hath said, out of his belly flow rivers of living water. (But spake he of the spirit, which they that believe on him should receive. For the Holy Ghost was not yet given, because that Jesus was not yet glorified".

The coming of Jesus became a guarantee and also a promise from God the father that the Holy Ghost will be given to those that believe in Christ Jesus. The Holy Ghost will now dwell in the life of such person on daily basis. John 16:7 – "Nevertheless I tell you the truth, it is expedient for you that I go away: for if I go not away, the comforter will not come unto you, but if I depart, I will send him unto you".

The Holy Ghost is one of the greatest blessings that we receive as we receive Christ. But we will also receive the baptism of the Holy Ghost when we conscientiously ask for him and thereafter we will experience the benefits of having Him in us.

(m) **<u>LIBERTY</u>**

In Gal. 2:4 We read - "And that because of false brethren unawares brought in, who came in privily to spy out <u>our liberty</u> which we have in Christ, that they might bring us into bondage".

Actually the moment we receive Jesus into our life there is a spiritual translation that immediately takes place. We will automatically be spiritually translated from the kingdom of darkness where we have been in bondage to the kingdom of Jesus, where we receive our liberty.

Jesus also announced this to us among wonderful blessings we shall receive as we receive him into our life in Luke 4:18 – " The spirit of the Lord is upon me because he hath anointed me to preach gospel to the poor, he hath sent me to heal the broken hearted, to preach deliverance to the captives, and recovering of sight to blind, to set at liberty them that are bruised". In whatever thing the devil had held you in bondage you shall receive liberty as you receive Jesus.

(n)   **<u>TRIUMPH</u>**

In 2 Cor. 2:14 We read – "Now thanks be unto God, which always causeth us to triumph in Christ, and maketh manifest the savior of his knowledge by us in every place".

When Jesus was coming into Jerusalem He knew it will be at Jerusalem that He will be arrested and crucified, but He carried out a prophetic action that announced to the people and the kingdom of darkness that whatever conspiracy or agenda they have against Him He will definitely triumph over them.

That is why we had triumphant entry of Jesus into Jerusalem and He also left Jerusalem triumphantly by overcoming devil and it's agents by his death on the cross.

Since then Jesus had earned us the privilege and grace to triumph over every situation that is working against us either in our marriage, health, finance or spiritual life. So we are now destined to triumph over the cross or false accusation from people.

There are many blessings that are associated with the coming of our Lord Jesus Christ.

The pages of this book may be small for us to exhaust all blessings Jesus has secured for us when He came and died.

But as we receive Him and walk in Him by the spirit and not by the flesh we will then experience all the blessings that are in Christ Jesus.

But I advise you that let not your purpose of coming to Jesus be solely for the blessings that you will receive in him. Jesus alone is far greater than blessings in Him. He is a personality that you will be glad to have. I am glad that God gave me the privilege and grace to have Jesus in my life.

CHAPTER TEN

HIS SECOND COMING

Acts 1:9:11 – "And when he had spoken these things, while they beheld, he was taken up, and a cloud received him out of their sight. And while they looked steadfastly toward heaven as he went up, behold two men stood by them in white apparel; which also said, ye men of Galilee, why stand ye gazing up into heaven? This same Jesus, which is taken up from you into heaven, shall so come in like manner as ye have seen him go into heaven".

The second coming of our Lord Jesus Christ is going to be two fold. The first fold of His coming is what is called RAPTURE and the second fold of His coming is called THE SECOND ADVENT.

We shall look at scriptures that tend to support the above assertion. Concerning rapture, in 1Thess. 4:13- 18 – "But I would not have you to be ignorant, brethren, concerning them which are asleep, that ye sorrow not, even as others which have no hope. For if we believe that Jesus died and rose again, even so them also which sleep in Jesus will God bring with him. For this we say unto you by the word of the Lord, that we which are alive and remain unto the coming of the Lord shall not prevent them which are asleep. For the Lord himself shall descend from heaven with a shout, with the voice of the arch angel, and with the trump of God, and the dead in Christ shall rise first: then we which are alive remain shall be caught up together with them in the clouds to meet the Lord in the air, and so shall we ever be with the Lord. Wherefore comfort one another with these words".

Concerning the second Advent we can observe a little difference from the rapture as we look at Matt. 24:29-31 – "Immediately after the tribulation of those days shall the sun be darkened and the moon shall not give her light, and stars shall fall from heaven, and the powers of the heavens shall be shaken. And then shall appear the sign of the son of man in heaven: and then shall all the tribes of the earth mourn, and they shall see the son of man coming in the clouds of heaven with power and great glory. And he shall send his angels with a great sound of a trumpet, and they shall gather together his elect from the four winds from one end of heaven to the other".

The purpose of this book is not to go into complete details about the second coming of our Lord Jesus Christ but just to highlight it as to remind us that Jesus is coming again. We need to prepare at all time since we don't know when He will come.

(A)   **<u>RAPTURE</u>**
Rapture as a word cannot be found in the Bible just like the word Trinity but they are all coined word to describe a thing or an event. In the case of rapture we can deduce its meaning from the bible to describe a spiritual occurrence prior to the second coming of our Jesus Christ.

Rapture has been described as a sudden momentary rising up, snatching away up into glory of believers who were dead first and those who are alive into the air to meet with the Lord Jesus Christ. See 1 Thess 4:16-17 – "..and the dead in Christ shall rise first: Then we which are alive and remain shall be caught up together with them in the clouds to meet the Lord in the air: and so shall we ever be with the Lord in the air.

The event of rapture will also include the transformation and translation of believers from the physical form on earth to be with the Lord without having the need to die. 1 Cor. 15:51 – 54. "Behold, I shew you a mystery; we shall not all sleep, but we shall be changed, in a moment, in the twinkling of an eye, at the last trump: for the trumpet shall sound, and the dead shall be raised incorruptible, and we shall be changed. For this corrupt corruptible must put on incorruption, and this mortal must put on immorality. So when this incorruptible shall have put on incorruption, and this mortal shall have put on immortality, then shall be brought to pass the saying that is written, death is swallowed up in victory".

The most important aspect of this event is that it is not your power to take yourself up and it is not in the hand of your pastor, General Overseer, or any man to decide whether you will be rapturable or not. When you meet with the conditions of God His power will be there to transform and translate you to meet with Jesus in the air. Note also that physical means like aeroplane will not be useful to assist anybody to get into the air.

Moreover the air being spoken of here is far beyond the height an aircraft can get to. For those who are in the aircraft that are qualified will also translate and get into the air from the aircraft just like the man in the valley at the time of rapture.

Rapture is also our meeting point with him in the air so nobody will have opportunity to bribe himself through or have the opportunity to receive human approval or connection to be among the raptured

Rapture is real and we cannot predict when it will take place but according to the scripture it shall precede the great tribulation so it requires us to work out our salvation with fear and trembling so that we escape the great tribulation.

(B)   <u>**THE SECOND ADVENT**</u>

This event describes the second fold of the second coming of Jesus Christ. Rev. 19:11 – 15 "And I sa heaven opened, and behold a white horse, and he that sat upon him was called faithful and true, and in righteousness he doth judge and make war. His eyes were as a flame of fire, and on his head were many crowns, and he had a name written, that no man knew, but he himself. And he was clothed with a vesture dipped in blood, and his name is called the word of God. And the armies which were in heaven followed him upon white horses, clothed in fine linen, white and clean. And out of his mouth goeth a sharp sword, that with it he should smite the nations: and he shall rule them with a rod of iron and he treadeth the winepress of the fierceness and wrath of Almighty God."

The second advent will be an event when Jesus will come not just to take the saints but no execute God's judgment.

This second advent will witness among other things as the scriptures said in Matt. 25:31 – 32 – "When the son of man shall come in his glory and all the holy angels with him, then shall he sit upon the throne of his glory: and before him shall be gathered all nations: and he shall separate them one from another, as a shepherd divideth his sheep from the goats". It is a time of separation among those that will be left, who did not rapture like the other saints.

In Jude 14, 15 ".. Behold, the Lord cometh with ten thousands of his saint to execute judgment upon all and to convince all that are ungodly among them all their ungodly deeds which they ungodly committed, and of their hard speeches which ungodly sinners have spoken against him". Also in 2 Thess. 7:7-10, 2:8.

Apart from executing judgment there are other things that Jesus will accomplished by his coming as we can see in Dan. 7:13, 14 "..behold one like the son of man came with the clouds of heaven, and came to the ancient of days and they brought him near before him. And there was given him dominion, and glory, and a kingdom, that all people, nations and languages, should serve him.." Jesus is coming to be served by all nations. The nations that refuse to serve Him now will eventually serve Him later.

Apart from the nations that will serve Jesus, there are those nations that will fight when He comes, See Zech. 14:3 – "Then shall the LORD go forth, and fight against those nations, as when fought in the day of battle".

Concerning rapture and the Second Advent, the scriptures that apply to one do not apply to the other. Not one passage refers to both events as if they were one. The rapture is first fold of the second coming, not a coming to earth but in the air. It could not be the Second Advent because Christ does not come to the earth to live here and fulfill a mission as He did at the first advent. When Christ meets the saints in the air, He takes them back to heaven with Him and presents them before the father's throne where they remain during the time the tribulation is running its course on the earth. See 1 Thess. 3:13.

Christ does not remain in the air with the saints when they meet him as in 1 Thess. 4:13 – 17. The marriage supper and the judgment of saints take place in heaven, then at the Second Advent after the tribulation, Christ and the saints leave heaven together to come down to the earth – See 2 Cor. 5:10 and Rev. 19.

The rapture is the time Christ comes for the saints to take them to heaven while the Second Advent is the time He comes to the earth to live here and fulfill a mission as enumerated above. This is the time He comes from heaven with the saints that have been raptured.

EVENTS THAT WILL HERALD HIS SECOND COMING

the rapture can take place any moment without anything being fulfilled. See 1 Cor. 15;51-52 – "Behold, I shew you a mystery, we shall not all sleep, but we shall all be changed, in a moment, in the twinkling of an eye, at the last trump: for the trumpet shall sound, and the dead shall be raised uncorruptible, and we shall be changed".

Though there will be no previous event as to make the saints get ready or know that rapture will soon take place but on the day of rapture some things will happen with quick succession that before people understand what is happening rapture has taken place. See 1 Thess. 4:16 – "For the Lord himself shall descend from heaven with a shout, with the voice of the archangel, and with the trump of God: and the dead in Christ shall rise first".

What the whole world shall be entitled to receive on this fateful day is the last trump of God the trumpet that shall sound the Lord's shout, and the voice of the archangel. It is better if you want to be raptured you don't need to wait for any event, if you do you will definitely miss the rapture because it is going to be a sudden occurrence which nobody knows when it will occur. It means it can occur today, tomorrow or while you are reading this book or before you drop this book. Why not stop now and put things in order by giving your life to Jesus or rededicating your life or decide to live a righteous life. The choice is yours.

While the Second Advent cannot take place until certain events have taken place. Note it must be after the tribulations. We shall then consider some few events in brief that will herald the second advent that is the second coming of Jesus that will usher in his coming on the earth to fulfill certain missions. Such events are as follows:

(a) **Deception:** Matt. 24:4-5 – "And Jesus answered and said unto them take heed that no man deceive you. For many shall come in my name, I am Christ, and shall deceive many".

(b) **False Christs And False Prophets:** Matt. 24:5 – "For many shall come in my name, saying I am Christ, and shall deceive many .. for there shall arise false Christ and false prophets, and shall shew great signs and wonders in so much that if it were possible, they shall deceive the very elect.

(c) **Wars and rumors of wars:** Matt. 24:6 – "And ye shall hear of wars and rumors of wars: see that ye be not troubled: for all these things must come to pass, but the end is not yet".

(d) **Famine, Earthquake And Pestilence:** See Matt. 24:7 – "For nation shall rise against nation, and kingdom against: and there shall be famines, pestilence, and earth quakes in divers places".

(e) **Hatred and Offences:** as in Matt. 24:10 – "And Then shall many be offended, and shall betray one another, and shall hate one another".

(f) **Iniquity Shall abound And Love Of Many Decreased:** See Matt. 24:12 – "And because iniquity shall abound, the love of many shall wax cold".

(g)   Increased Gospel Work: See Matt. 24:14 – "And this gospel of the kingdom shall be preached in all the world for a witness unto all nations and then shall the end come".

(h)   Abomination Of Desolation: See Matt. 24:15 – "When ye therefore shall see the abomination of desolation spoken of by Daniel the prophet, stand in the holy place (whose readeth, let him understand)".

(i)   Increase Sex Offences And Sex Perversion: Matt.24:38-39 – "For as in the days that were before the flood they were eating and drinking, marrying and giving in marriage, until the day that Noah entered into the ark. And knew not until the flood came, and took them all away, so shall also the coming of the son of man be".

(j)   Great Tribulation: Which shall last for 3½ years. In Matt. 24:21- "For then shall be great tribulation, such as was not since the beginning of the world to this time, no, nor ever shall be".

(k)   Martyrdoms: In Matt. 24:9 – "Then shall they deliver you up to be afflicted, and shall kill you: and ye shall be hated of all nations for my name's sake".

(l)   Increase Satanic Power Manifestation: In Matt. 24:24 "For there shall arise false Christs, and false prophets, and shall shew great signs and wonders, insomuch that, if it were possible, they shall deceive the very elect".

(m) **Moon, Sun And Stars Affected:** Matt. 24:29 – "Immediately after the tribulation of those days shall the sun be darkened, and the moon shall not give light, and the stars shall fall from heaven, and the powers of the heavens shall be shaken".

There are other events as recorded in the scripture which shall serve as a pointer to the Second Advent of our Lord Jesus Christ. The most important thing is not to wait and be counting the events that have taken place as to use head knowledge to know when the time for His second coming is here.

We cannot know the exact hour when Jesus shall come. See Matt. 24:36 – "But of that day and hour knoweth no man, no not the angels of heaven, but my father only".

The best we can do for ourselves is to make sure we are qualified to be raptured now that we have the privilege, for Jesus said "except that the days of tribulation is shortened no man would have been able to be saved".

THE PURPOSE OF RAPTURE

In 1 Thess. 4"16-17 – "For the Lord himself shall descend from heaven with a shout, with the voice of the archangel, and with the trump of God: and the dead in Christ shall rise first: Then we which are alive and remain shall be caught up together with them in the clouds to meet the Lord in the air and so shall we ever be with the Lord"

We shall briefly look at some of the purposes of rapture:
    (1) To receive believers to himself as he promised during his earthly ministry. See John 14:1-3 – Let not your heart be troubled: ye believe in God, believe also in me.

In my father's house there are many mansions. If it were not so, I would have told you. I go to prepare a place for you and if I go and prepare a place for you, I will come again, and receive you unto myself, that where I am, there ye may be also".

(2)   To resurrect the dead in Christ among the dead so that the purpose of God for saving them may be fulfilled. See 1 Thess. 4:14 – "For if we believe that Jesus died and rose again, even so them also which sleep in Jesus will God bring with him".

(3)   To remove the saints from the world before the great tribulation come upon the world. Luke 21:34-36 – "and take heed to yourselves, lest at any time your hearts be overcharged with surfeiting, and drunkenness, and cares of this life, and so that day come upon you unawares. For as a snare shall it come on all them that dwell on the face of the whole earth. Watch ye therefore, and pray always, that ye may be counted worthy to escape all these things that shall come to pass, and to stand before the son of man".

(4)   To take believer to live in the New Jerusalem in heaven and to receive rewards. Heb 12:22-23 – "But ye are come unto mount Zion, and unto the city of the living God, the heavenly Jerusalem, and to an innumerable company of angels. To the general assembly and church of the first born, which are written in heaven and to God the judge of all, and to the spirits of just men made perfect". Also in 2 Cor. 5:10 – "For we must all appear before the judgment seat of Christ: that every one may receive the things done in his body, according to that he hath done, whether it be good or bad".

(5)   To change the bodies of believers from mortality to immortality – Phil. 3":1 "Who shall change our vile body, that it may be fashioned like unto his glorious body, according to the working whereby he is able even to subdue all things unto himself" See 1 Cor. 15:35-58.

(6)   To present believers before God. Jude 24 – "Now unto him that is able to keep his glory from falling and to present you before the presence of his glory with exceeding joy".

(7)   To assemble the believers at the marriage supper of the Lamb Rev. 19:7 – "Let us be glad and rejoice, and give honour to him: for the marriage of the lamb is come, and his wife hath made herself ready".

(8)   That Jesus might present it to himself a glorious church not having spot, or wrinkle, or any such thing, but that it should be holy and without blemish".

(9)   To permit the revelation and manifestation of the Anti Christ 2 Thess. 2;6 - 8 – "And now ye know what witholdeth that he might be revealed in his time. For the mystery of iniquity doth already work only he who now letteh will let. Until he be taken out of the way. And then shall that wicked be reveled whom the Lord shall consume with the spirit of his mouth, and shall destroy with the brightness of his coming".

<u>QUALIFICATION FOR RAPTURE</u>

(a)   **<u>Born Again:</u>** Except a man is born again he cannot see the kingdom of God – John 3:3. The first and the most important condition to qualify to partake in the rapture whether dead or alive is you must be Born Again.

(b)   **<u>Those Who Abide In Him</u>**: It is just not enough to be born again and thereafter forsake Jesus. May be you were in a meeting by the influence of the Holy Spirit you were touched by the message and you gave your life to Jesus and thereafter continued your former life as if nothing happened. You must remain in Christ till the time of your death or rapture. John 15:6 – "If a man abide not in me, he is cast forth as a branch, and is withered, and men gather them, and cast them into the fire, and they are burned".

(c)   **<u>Holiness:</u>** Holiness is a sine qua non for you to be raptured dead or alive so it not what any believer will play with it Heb. 12:14 – "Follow peace with all men and holiness without which no man shall see the Lord". Since rapture entails seeing the Lord it is important we are holy so that we can see him.

(d)   **<u>Those Who Desire His appearing And Prepare For It:</u>** 2 Tim.4:8 "Hence forth there is laid up for me a crown of righteousness, which the Lord, the righteousness judge, shall give me at that day: and not to me only, but unto all them also that love his appearing".

(e)   **<u>Those That Keep His Commandment:</u>** Obedience to the commandment of God is important if we must rapture. 1 Tim. 6:4 "That thou keep this commandment without spot, unrebukeable, until the appearing of our Lord Jesus Christ".

<u>THE PURPOSE OF THE SECOND ADVENT – THE MILLENNIAL REIGN OF 1000 YEARS</u>

In 1 Cor. 15:24-28 – "Then cometh the end, when he shall have delivered up the kingdom to God even the father, when he shall have put down all rule, and all authority and power, for he   must reign, till he hath put all enemies under his feet. The last enemy that shall be destroy is death. For he hath put all things under his feet. But when he saith all things are put under him, it is manifest that he is accepted, which did put all things under him. And when all things shall be subdued unto him then shall the son also himself be subject unto him that put all things under him, that God may be all in all".

(1)   Jesus must deliver the millennial kingdom to God See 1 Cor. 15:24.

(2)   All rebellious rule, authority and power must be put down by Jesus during this millennial kingdom. It is obvious we should not accuse God of being silence when things are going wrongly in our nations because there is a set time when such rebellion must be crushed by Jesus whom God had appointed to do the job for him.

(3)   Death had in the past tormented the world and held even some believers in constant torment of fear. Sometimes when we remember how a believer was crushed by the power of death sometimes untimely we could imagine our hearts filled with sorrows. But the good news is that Jesus must destroy death during this millennial reign see 1 Cor. 15:26 – "The last enemy that shall be destroyed is death.

(4)   Jesus work or ridding the earth of rebellion must be accomplished and accepted by our heavenly father who by divine arrangement has assigned this job to our Lord Jesus. God the father is all ready waiting to receive this report. We remember that when Jesus came for his earthly ministry He also gave God His earthly report as recorded in John Chapter 17 and after His death He

went to heaven to present His work accomplished on the cross to God. God is still waiting for the last report of accomplishment which must come at the end of the millennial reign of Jesus.

Finally, God becomes all and all again. Restoration of the whole order both in heaven and on earth back to God as it was in the beginning before the heavenly rebellion by Lucifer and earthly rebellion by Adam.

THE EFFECTS OR RESULTS OF THE MILLENNIAL REIGN OF JESUS

The millennial reign of Jesus indeed shall be a blessing to all believers who endured in the end and it will be the right time to answer the question the apostles of Jesus asked him before his ascension to heaven.

In Acts 1:6, 7 We read – "When they therefore were together, they asked of him, saying, Lord, wilt thou at this time restore the kingdom to Israel? And he said unto them, it is not for you to know the times or seasons, which the father hath put in his own power".

The millennial reign, will not only restore the kingdom of Israel but it will no longer be a restoration meant for only physical Israel but the spiritual Israel those who by faith in Jesus Christ have become the seed of Abraham now called believers.

The millennial reign can also be described as the reign of the righteous. It will be a season when some believers will be given some cities or nations to rule or govern. The millennial reign of Jesus will so include the new Jerusalem coming down from heaven on earth and the righteous shall enjoy eternal bliss see Rev. 21:1 – 5 = "And I saw heaven and a new earth: for the first heaven and first earth were passed away and there was no more sea.. New Jerusalem coming down from God out of heaven, prepared as a bride adorned for her husband. And I heard a great voice out of heaven saying, behold, the tabernacle of God is with men, and he will dwell with them, and they shall be his people, and God himself shall be with them, and be their God. And God shall wipe away all tears from their eyes, and there shall be no more death, neither sorrow, nor crying, neither shall there be any more pain: for the former things are passed away. And he that sat upon the throne said, behold, I make all things new. And he said me, write: for these words are true and faithful".

The above are not words of excitement but promises our God had made for the righteous. These promises are only meant for those who shall be qualified for it Rev. 21:6 – 7 – "And he said unto me, it is done. I am Alpha and Omega, the beginning and the end. I will give unto him that is athirst of the founta of the water of life freely. He that overcome shall inherit all things and I will be his God, and he shall be my son".

Apart from the above promises stated in the scriptures quoted above there are other things Jesus will do during his millennial reign which we can enumerate as follows:

    (a)   Judge the people in righteousness
    (b)   Deliver the poor from oppression
    (c)   Judge the poor in justice
    (d)   Cause the righteous to flourish
    (e)   Completely defeat his enemies
    (f)   Redeem souls from deceit and violence
    (g)   Receive praise from the people
    (h)   Bless men eternally
    (i)   Save the children of the needy
    (j)   Rule with universal dominion
    (k)   Give succor to the helpless
    (l)   Giver the rightcous the power to live eternally
    (m)   IIe will destroy the oppressors and there are other things too.

CHAPTER ELEVEN

HOW YOU CAN RECEIVE JESUS IN YOUR LIFE

In John 1:12 "But as many as received him, to them gave he power to become the sons of God, even to them that believe on his name".

Further in John 3:3, 7 We read – "Jesus answered and said unto him, verily, verily, I say unto thee, except a man be born again, he cannot see the kingdom of God. Marvel not that I said unto thee, ye must be born again".

The question that readily faces any person arc there relationship between "receiving Jesus", believing" in him and "being born again"? Are they saying the same thing? Do they mean the same thing?.

A lot of confusion has been set in the mind of many people and some don't understand what it means to be born again. Though the answer here may not be authoritative but at least might enlighten us towards understanding the meaning of those three phrases receiving Jesus, believing in him and being born again.

I believe that the three phrases are saying the same thing meaning that they are talking about a relationship that is established between a person and Jesus by fulfilling any of those phrases mentioned above. For it to be said that you arc born again you must have believed the message of Jesus Christ and thereafter received him into your life by that simple prayer of salvation. Once you have done that Heaven and even the earth will record it for you that you are born again.

From the scriptures we read above, it is only when you have either believed in him after hearing and receiving the message of Jesus Christ or you have received him into your life after believing his message that power can be given to you by God to become His sons (children).

In our present time Christianity though not a religion, has been regarded as an accepted religion and such confession of Jesus as the son of God has become a mere form in many churches. Some think that because they acknowledge this fact in public they are saved from sin and are true Christians. One can do this only mentally and with the tongue many times a day without having a change in his life. That is why today there are so many people who have confessed of Jesus publicly without a corresponding change in their lifestyle. Unless a change in the person's lifestyle is effected, the real baptism of the Holy Ghost that will help the person in his Christian race will not be there. Moreover, unless one makes a conscious effort to establish a close relationship with Jesus Christ, there can be no change in his lifestyle.

As long as the confession of Jesus publicly is performed by the person as to fulfill all righteousness or as an exercise of mental activity the baptism of the Holy Ghost cannot take place in the person's life. The condition under which the Holy Ghost will dwell in the life of any person is that he must be born again and his name is now found in the book of life by the Holy Ghost before He comes to dwell in that person.

Being born again or being a believer does not end with exercising the tongue in that direction. Rather it starts from the heart and ends with the mouth. If it does not start from the heart and end with the mouth , it is not assafe to say that the person is born again or is a believer.

One must believe from the heart as well as confess with the mouth see Rom. 10:10 "That if thou shall confess with thy mouth the

Lord Jesus and shalt believe in thine heart that God hath raised him from the dead, and with the mouth confession is made unto salvation".

It is important to note that before we come out to make a public confession of Jesus as our personal savior and Lord, we must allow our heart to receive the conviction of the Holy Ghost so that we can see our emptiness without Jesus.

The moment the person believe in his heart and follows it up with a confession of the mouth in the acknowledgment of Jesus as the only begotten son of God who came in the flesh and died for our sins and thereby becoming a ground or basis that we are receiving him into our heart as our Lord and personal savior, he will automatically become a new creature in Christ Jesus – 2 Cor. 5:17 – "Therefore if any man be in Christ, he is new creature, old things are passed away, behold, all things are become new".

The true confession and receiving Jesus into one's life includes complete surrender of one's life to God and with serious consecration regarding future conduct that will be according to the whole will of God – Rom. 12:2 – "I beseech you therefore, brethren, by the mercies of God, that ye present your bodies a living sacrifice, holy acceptable unto God, which is your reasonable service. And be not conformed to this world: but by the renewing of your mind that ye may prove what is that good, and acceptable, and perfect will of God".

You confess Jesus as personal savior and Lord and your heart was not part of it you have not fulfilled the scripture that will enable you be regarded as a born again Christian and you have also denied yourself the power from God that will make you to be one of the children of God.

The unfortunate thing about the situation above is that the world including the Christendom will look at you as a born again

Christian or believer while haven has no record of your name in the book of life.

While other believers know that their expectations shall not be cut off because God is their father and heaven is backing up their expectation, the person who did not fulfill the scriptural requirement, will definitely be cut off by the devil who also knows that he is not among the covenant children of God. For God is only interested in those who already have a covenant with Him though the sacrifice of our Lord Jesus. Ps. 50:5 – "Gather my saints together unto me, those that have a covenant with me by sacrifice".

It is only those that have complied with God's instruction that God is interested to help or save whenever they are in need. Ps. 50:15 – "And call upon me in the day of trouble, I will deliver thee, and thou shall glorify me".

<u>NECESSITY OF BEING BORN AGAIN</u>

We have seen that it is necessary that we must be born again. When we look at John 3:3 we see one of the necessities of being born again.

(1)   As in John 3:3 you cannot see the kingdom of God unless you are born again. If you have an alternative arrangement or believe that does not conform to God's commandment then it is obvious that you cannot see the kingdom of God which means literally that heaven is not a place for such a one. To be in heaven you must be born again.

(2)   According to John 1:12, it is important that one becomes born again that means by believing or receiving Jesus into his life as to receive power from God to become the sons of God. Since this power comes from God not from the Pastor or religious leader, there is no short cut or alternative to God's

commandment. If you fail to follow God's command, definitely, you will not receive the power to become the sons (children) of God.

(3) **Power To Do Righteousness:** 1 John 2:29 – "If ye know that he is righteous, ye know that every one that doeth righteousness is born of him". It is not just enough to be born again but there is need to maintain a righteous life as to qualify to make heaven. It is only when you are born again that you can receive power to do righteousness.

(4) **Freedom from Sin**: sin will remain a master to anybody that is not born again. Even when you are born again and you continue to live a life of sin you will also not make heaven. So in other to make heaven you need freedom from the bondage of sin 1 John 3:9 – "Whosoever is born of God doth not commit sin, for his seed remaineth in him: and he cannot sin, because he is born of God".

(5) **Power To Overcome The World:** The world has an influence that can make a believer live a compromised life thereby denying himself the benefit of making heaven. It is important that you are born again as to receive power to overcome the world and the lust thereof. 1 John5:4-5 – "For whatsoever is born of God overcometh the world: and this is the victory that overcometh the world, even our faith. Who is he that overcometh the world, but he that believeth that Jesus is the son of God?". Many have taken new year resolutions to stop some habits of the flesh like smoking, drinking, womanizing, pornography etc but those resolutions failed immediately it was taken. The only way to overcome the world is to believe in Jesus

Christ and as you do that be sure you must have a testimony.

(6)   **Baptism Of The Holy Ghost:** Acts 2:38-39 – "Then Peter said unto them, and be baptized everyone of you in the name of Jesus Christ for the remission of sins, and ye shall receive the gift of the Holy Ghost. For the promise is unto you, and to your children, and to all that are afar off, even as many as the Lord our God shall call". The only condition to receive the baptism of the Holy Ghost is by being born again. It is necessary so that you can have the Holy Ghost that will help you to live a victorious Christian life and receive a fulfillment of your expectation. There is no short cut to the baptism of Holy Ghost you must be born again.

(7)   **Love For God:** You cannot have the real love for God until you are born again. In 1 John 4:19 –"We love him, because he first loved us". 1 John 5:1 – "Whosoever believeth that Jesus is the Christ is born of God: and every one that loveth him that begat him also that is begotten of him". The love of God that keeps us going in our Christian race is necessary for our life.

(8)   **Love For Brethren:** The natural tendency of every man is to be selfish desiring to be loved without a correspondent love for others. So the power to love others selflessly comes by being born again. 1 John 5:2 – "By this we know that we love the children of God, when we love God, and keep his commandments".

(9)   **Power To Keep God's Commandment:** The power to keep God's commandment also comes from God alongside with the power to become his sons (children) when you believe in him or receive him. 1 John 5:3 – " For this is the love of God, that keep his

commandments: and his commandments are not grevious".

(10) **Freedom From Satan:** That you are now born again does not make the devil (Satan) to remove his focus on you rather his wrath increases against you but with being born again comes a freedom from the oppression and manipulations of Satan. 1 John 5:18 – "We know that whatsoever is born of God sinneth not, but he that is begotten of God keepeth himself, and that wicked one toucheth him not".

(11) **Sonship From God:** We can proudly announce to anybody that we are the sons of God which means the moment we are born again we become sons of God and the rights and privileges accruing to sons becomes ours immediately. 1 John3:1-3 – "Behold, what manner of love the father hath bestowed upon us, that we should be called the sons of God: Therefore the world knoweth us not, because it knew him not. Beloved, now are we the sons of God, and it doth not yet appear what shall be, but we know that, when he shall appear, we shall be like him, for we shall see him as he is. And every man hath this hope in him purifieth himself, even as he is pure".

<u>HOW CAN ONE RECEIVE HIM</u>

There are so many ways that people have written to show the way to receive Jesus into one's life. The procedures may not be the same but the content must be the same. What matters most is not the procedures you adopted or the prayer model used, the most important ingredients is the believing from the heart and confession that shall be unto salvation.

I shall adopt the very simple and rich procedure I saw in one of the voice magazine of Full Gospel Businessmen Fellowship

International, with permission, I shall likewise state it as simple as I saw it in the book.

(1)   **<u>Acknowledge:</u>**
Rom. 3:23 – "For all have sinned and come short of the glory of God". Also in PS. 51:5 – "Behold, I was shapen in iniquity, and in sin did my mother conceive me". So there is need for you to acknowledge that you are a sinner.

(2)   **<u>Repent:</u>**
Luke 13:3 – "Except you repent, you shall all likewise perish". Repentance is a sine qua non to be born again so that his sins will be blotted out. Acts 3:19 – "Repent ye therefore, and be converted that your sins may be blotted out". Repentance means turning away from your sins".

(3)   **<u>Confess:</u>**
Rom. 10:9 – "That if thou shalt confess with thy mouth the Lord Jesus, and shalt believe in thin heart that God hath raised him from the dead, thou shalt be saved".

(4)   **<u>Forsake:</u>**
When you have confessed Jesus as your Lord and personal Saviour you must forsake those wicked ways called sin. Isa. 55:7 – "Let the wicked forsake his way, and the unrighteous man his thoughts and let him return unto the Lord, and he will have mercy upon him, and to our God, for he will abundantly pardon".

(5)   **<u>Believe:</u>**
John 3:16 – "For God so loved the world, that he gave his only begotten son, that whosoever believeth in him should not perish, but have everlasting life".

(6)   **<u>Receive:</u>**
John 1:11 – 12 – "He came unto his own, and his own receiveth him not. But as many as received him, to them gave he power to become the sons of God.."

The essence of this chapter is to tell you the necessity to be born again and guide you into receiving Jesus Christ into your heart. If you are convicted in your heart to receive Jesus Christ you can meet any minister of the gospel that is born again and understands the need for one to be born again to pray for you.

In the alternative you may follow us and pray this prayer and allow the Holy Ghost to enlarge the prayer in your heart if he desires: **"Our heavenly father, I acknowledge that I am a sinner and that Jesus came in the flesh and died for the remission of my sins. Lord Jesus forgive me and come into my life, this day I believe in what you did at the cross of calvary and I want you into my life today as my Lord and personal Saviour. Give me the power to live a victorious Christian life so that eternal life shall be mine. Thank you for receiving me in Jesus name I pray – Amen".**

Congratulation if you have sincerely prayed this prayer. I also join my faith with yours and ask the heavenly father to receive you and enter your name in the book of life, in Jesus name – Amen.

If you have also backslidden you can as well pray the prayer and ask God for help to overcome the spirit of backsliding.

I know God will surely help you in Jesus name Amen.

CHAPTER TWELVE

CONSEQUENCES FOR REJECTING HIM

When Jesus came into this world, some received Him while others did not receive Him. From that time Jesus came and died and resurrected till now, many have received Him and some also have rejected Him.

John 1:11 – 12 – "He came unto his own, and his own received him not. But as many as received him, to them gave he power to become the sons of God, even to them that believe on his name".

The option to receive Jesus or reject him is only here on earth once you die the option will not be presented to you again. Heb. 9:27 – "And as it is appointed unto men once to die, but after this the judgment".

This judgment that is talked about here is a judgment that shall be based on the person's work while alive here on earth see Rev. 20:12 – "And I saw the dead. Small and great, stand before God; and the books were opened: and another book was opened which is the book of life: and the dead were judged out of those things which were written in the books according to their works".

So as you are still alive, you have option to accept or reject Jesus into your life. If you receive Him be sure eternal life is there waiting for you but if you reject Him there are consequences that must follow you due to your rejection of Him. Note it very well that if you don't call Him your Lord here on earth, over there in eternity you must call Him Lord. The consequences or refusal or failure to receive Jesus are as follows:

(a)   **<u>You Will Perish:</u>**
In John 3:16 – "For God so Love the world that he gave his only begotten son, that whosoever believeth in him should not perish, but have everlasting life".
God has made available unto us an everlasting life if you accept Jesus as your Lord, but in the alternative, there is perishing that is also reserved for those who do not receive or believe in Jesus Christ: Remember the perishing here apart from the body that will be affected, the soul of that person will also perish that means not having privilege to enjoy everlasting life after the person's death.

(b)   **<u>There Will Be Condemnation:</u>**
The condemnation you face when you are not born again starts from here and continue till when you die unless you stop the condemnation before you die.

In John 3;18-19 – "He that believeth on him is not condemned: but he that believeth not is condemned already, because he hath not believed in the name of the only begotten son of God. And this is the condemnation, that light is come into the world, and men loved darkness rather than light, because their deeds were evil".

Also Rom. 8:1. As long as you are in Christ Jesus there is no condemnation for you but if you reject Jesus or refuse to be born again for whatever reason you may have, definitely you have brought condemnation unto yourself.

(c)   **<u>The Wrath Of God:</u>**
In John 3:36 – "He that believeth on the son hath everlasting life, and he that believeth not the son shall not see life, <u>but wrath of God abideth on him</u>".

I don't think anybody can stand the wrath of God. If you refuse to believe in Jesus by being born again as Jesus demanded in John 3:3, 7, definitely you must attract the wrath of God upon yourself. Note Heb. 10:31 "It is a fearful thing to fall into the hands of the living God".

To avoid falling into God's hand and attracting his wrath, you better give your life to Jesus. If you fall into the hand of man or woman God may rescue you, if you call upon him but if you fall into the hand of God by reason of his wrath upon you who then can rescue you?.

(d)   **<u>No Life For You:</u>**
Jesus made a promise in John 10:10 that you will have life and have it in abundance but where you reject Him then you will not see life or have it. See John 3:36 "He that believeth on the son hath everlasting life, and he that <u>believeth not the son shall not see life</u>"...
Why you will not see life or have it is in John 3:35 – "The father loveth the son, and hath given all things into his hand".

(e)   **<u>No Fruit Bearing:</u>**
In John 15:4 – "Abide in me and I in you. As the branch cannot bear fruit of itself, except it abide in the vine, no more can ye, except ye abide in me".

There are spiritual fruits you are required to bear and there are material fruits you are expected to produce. If you don't abide in Christ and He abides in you both spiritual and material fruits cannot come from you.

(f)   **<u>Damnation:</u>**

In Mark 16:16 – "He that believeth and is baptized shall be saved, but he that believeth not shall be damned".

There is a damnation for those who reject Jesus in this life. If you refuse Jesus coming into your life as Lord and personal Saviour you have by choice, brought damnation upon your life.

Be sure that if you bring damnation upon your life you have directly invited curse upon yourself. Definitely you will not excel no matter how you try. You may gather in quantum one day the devil will still come to scatter because there is a damnation upon your life.

(g)   **<u>Cast Into the Lake of Fire:</u>**
In Rev. 20:15 – "And whosoever was not found written in the book of life was cast into the lake of fire".

The worst thing that will happen to anybody is to come to this world and go to hell but the hell that is made of lake of fire. Remember that your stay in this lake of fire is not just for a year or 100 years then come out. No, it is just eternity i.e forever. You have a choice now to avoid this lake of fire by doing what Jesus said you must do.

We know today the universities have their requirements into their institution no matter how connected you are to the Vice chancellor if you do not want to suffer disgrace at the end of your academic career you will insist and ensure that you meet up the requirements.
Even if you are the son of the Vice Chancellor you must meet with the standard because it can be used against you in the future.

God has set his own standard to qualify you entering the kingdom of God the father and that requirement must be met if you must escape these consequences and make heaven. That requirement is found in John 3:3, 7 which was expatiated in Rom. 10:9, 10 – "He said you must be born again for you to see the kingdom of God.

Our prayer and desire is not that these consequences the scripture has outlined should fall upon you rather that you can escape it now.

When Moses was about to die he told the Israelites in Deu. 30:19 – "I call heaven and earth to record this day against you, that I have set before you life and death, blessing and cursing: therefore choose life that both thou and thy seed may live".

Please choose life that is in Jesus so that you may live and have everlasting life.

CHAPTER THIRTEEN

WHO THEN IS THIS JESUS?

In conclusion we have gotten a little knowledge about who Jesus is. I know the knowledge put down in this book is not enough but the Holy Spirit will enlarge your understanding concerning who Jesus is.

The revelation knowledge of who Jesus is will change your world view and bring a change in your life that no power can withstand you.

You will discover that Jesus in you is the hope of glory. you will not be afraid of the future neither will you be afraid of any person, power, principalities or demonic kingdom because you will know that He (Jesus) that is in you is greater than he that is in the world as in 1 John 4:4.

There are many divine knowledge or revelation we can derive from statements made about Jesus in the scripture.

The purpose of this chapter is not to start from the beginning to study who Jesus is but to bring out some important statement made about him which the Holy Spirit given the opportunity will use to enlighten us.

In Matt. 3;17 – " And lo a voice from heaven, saying, this is my beloved son, in whom I am well pleased".

This statement was made by God concerning Jesus during Jesus Baptism by John the Baptist.

Also in Matt. 17:5 – "While he yet spake, behold, a bright cloud overshadowed them: and behold a voice out of the cloud, which said, this is my beloved son in whom I am well pleased; hear ye him". This was God's statement concerning Jesus during Jesus transfiguration on the mountain.

I just want you to ponder on this particular statement made by John the Baptist concerning Jesus. I believe as you do that the Holy Spirit will give you deeper knowledge and understanding of whom Jesus is.

But before we consider the statement of John the Baptist concerning Jesus, we need to consider Jesus statement about John the Baptist so that we know that John was not just a mean man, he was a man that had good credentials before God and his statement should be given due consideration.

In Luke 7:24, 26 & 28 – "And when the messenger of John were departed, he began to speak unto the people concerning John, what went ye out into the wilderness for to see? A reed shaken with the wind?... But what went ye out for to see? A prophet yea, I say unto you, and much more than a prophet.. for I say unto you, among those that are born of women there is not a greater prophet than John the Baptist: but he that is least in the kingdom of God is greater than he".

Among all that have come into this world through women none can be compared with John the Baptist. We know apart from Adam God created and Melchizedek the priest of the Most High God every other person passed through a woman.

It then means from all the great men of the Bible like Noah, Abraham, Isaac, Jacob, Daniel, Elijah, David, Moses, Joshua, Samuel etc. none can be compared in level or greatness to John the Baptist.

It is then this same John the Baptist whom Heaven adjudged as the greatest that now made this statement about Jesus in Matt. 3:11 – "In indeed I baptize you with water unto repentance: but he that cometh after me is mightier than I, whose shoes I am not worthy to bear: he shall baptize you with the Holy ghost with fire".

If John the Baptist who is the greatest of all people born by woman is telling us that Jesus is mightier than him and he is not worthy to bear or carry Jesus shoes. I don't even know if I am qualified to just look at Jesus. But praise be to God who has given us the privilege not just to bear His shoes or touch His garment but this Jesus lives in us. He lives in me.

There was no other way for John the Baptist to describe Jesus than to make a flat statement so that the Holy Spirit can broaden our understanding on whom Jesus is.

Any day you understand a little of whom Jesus is, your life will never remain the same. The power to understand who Jesus is cannot be given to you until you have believed in Him or received Him into your life as Lord and personal Saviour and you continue to serve Him in truth and spirit then you will also be given the power to become the son of God.

Once the power is given the Holy Ghost can now come to explain Jesus to you and bring glory to Jesus. My only advice to you is receive Jesus into your life as your Lord and personal Saviour (i.e) be born again. You will have Him full in your life. Note life without Christ is crises.

Congratulation as you take this honourable decision to be born again and serve him in truth and spirit.